Discernment

DISCERNMENT

Kirby & Sandra Clements

Foreword by Dr. Kelley Varner

CLEMENTS
MINISTRIES

Decatur, GA

Discernment
Copyright 2016 Dr. Kirby Clements Sr. and Sandra Clements

Address inquiries to the publisher:

Clements Family Ministry
2000 Cathedral Place
Decatur, Georgia 30034 USA

Learn more about the authors and their ministry at www.clementsministries.org

ISBN: 978-0-9968702-5-2 (print)
ISBN: 978-0-9794181-7-4 (ebook)

LCCN: 2018741311

First Printing: 1999
Second Printing: 2018

Printed in the United States of America

Edited by Annette R. Johnson

Dedication

To my son, Kirby Jr., a keen discerner of truth.
My special thanks to the late Archbishop Earl Paulk Jr., who con-
stantly reminded his audiences through the years that the "mark of
maturity" is discernment. This statement alone served as the motivation
for this work.

Acknowledgements

My gratitude and thanks to the following people for their time and energy dedicated to the completion of this work:

Charlotte Lemons

Connie Raiford

Barb Rarden

Annyce Stone

Table of Contents

Foreword

The present mandate of the Holy Spirit upon every Christian leader is to "*[equip] the saints for the work of ministry...till we all come to...a perfect ["complete, full-grown"] man...that we should no longer be children, tossed to and fro and carried about with every wind of doctrine...*" (Eph. 4:12-14, NKJ)

One of my mentors, Archbishop Earl Paulk of Atlanta, teaches that the peculiarity of the mature Church is discernment. The Greek noun for "discernment" means "perception." It is derived from a word that means "to apprehend properly." The Greek verb is "diakrino," and it literally means "to judge through."

This anticipated volume, "Discernment," by Dr. Kirby and Sandra Clements does just that. Like the apostolic team of Aquila and Priscilla, they have cut through the religious fat to prophesy to our generation and the generations to come. God has armored them spiritually and scholastically to bring this much-needed word of clear instruction to all peoples and nations.

After calling us to maturity, they define and align biblical discernment with the real world, the invisible realm of spirit, making a clear distinction between spiritual activity in the kingdom of darkness and the Kingdom of God. They join their veteran ministerial experience with an insightful awareness of historical attitudes to educate us with regard to natural issues. The prophet and prophetess then communicate how to understand and judge prophetic utterances. Chapter Six, which explains the differences between reformation, refreshing, and religious fads, is classic. The closing sections explore the practicality of body life working through the instrumentality of His Church as we move forward in the purpose of His Kingdom. Their summary and concluding examples furnish the pragmatic platform from which we all can implement their wisdom.

In a day when younger ministers are falling prey to Rehoboam's folly of rejecting the seasoned advisement of the elders (I Kings 12: 6-8), we would be prudent to heed their godly wisdom.

The Holy Ghost is like a river, but He always flows between banks. He has direction and purpose. "Discernment" is required reading for every Christian, whether parent or pastor. These proven principles will help guide us through perilous times into the global harvest of the twenty-first century Church.

-Dr. Kelley Varner
Senior Pastor
Praise Tabernacle, Richlands, NC

CHAPTER 1

Understanding the Call to Discernment

Human beings are complex creations, uniquely combining the spiritual, emotional, and physical in the expression of being. Understanding of the interrelationship of these components or natures is essential to the growth, development, and actualization of each. Life is experienced on physical and spiritual levels in the midst of competing forces: good vs. evil, life vs. death. Perception of this totality is necessary for right choices and appropriate actions.

A young man came to my office wanting to be delivered from what he called a "seducing spirit." He described his behavior and earnestly attributed all of his problems to the spirit world. When I suggested to him that his behavior was not totally rooted in spiritual oppression, we began to deal realistically with causes and solutions. Human beings are not without control of their behavior. Because we are rational and conscious beings, we have the power of choosing our courses in life. Our orientation in life may have conditioned our patterns, values, and concepts; however, we should not negate our power to change. Unrestrained sexual behavior may or may not be a spiritual problem, but it is evidence of the inability to exercise willpower.

From this example, we can clearly see that understanding of life, self, and others cannot be achieved without a "tool" for accurately sorting out complexities at every level in both the spiritual and physical realms. The Kingdom of God is awaiting the manifestation of the children of God. The return of Christ and the establishment of His rule and reign will follow the maturation of the whole body of Christ, the Bride. And maturation requires keen discernment.

The call of discernment at an individual level is the precursor to full maturation of the body of Christ. The individual believer must gain the skills and spiritual insight necessary to make proper decisions at every level of life. The Christian living in a world that is operating on a different set of principles and priorities must guard against conformity to these influences. Decisions about personal relationships, education, economics, and other social concerns must be directed by principles and precepts that do not cause estrangement from Biblical guidelines. The individual Christian must have his/her "organs of perception" well trained in order to distinguish between good and evil and to know times, seasons, and appropriate responses.

If there is to be unity of the body of Christ, then the vast population of individual Christians and corporate groups must be able to recognize the basis of our "oneness," which is Christ Jesus, while keeping our theological and doctrinal differences in a proper context. Many differences in beliefs and practices exist among the many membered Body of Christ. Many times these non-foundational differences become the basis of our disunity. However, by discerning the foundations of classical Christianity, the prayer of the Lord Jesus for unity will be realized.

We are faced today with numerous global trends in science, technology, religion, economics, politics, and popular culture. Emerging computer culture, changing family values, and distracting economic and political trends are all offering many new options to this fast food generation. How is this generation to participate in these ever-evolving currents of change? What is fundamental or classical to a Christian existence in such an evolving world? After all, language, symbols, values, and even principles are becoming "fuzzy." Absolute beliefs and fundamental precepts are being clouded by "relativism" and the numerous options opened to every global occupant. In the search for truth and for the right way, the questions are asked: "What is truth?" and "What is the right way?" Discernment, it would seem, is necessary in a broader context that can properly relate the Christian to this multidimensional world.

I earnestly believe that salvation and the ongoing work of the Holy Spirit in the life of the individual is absolutely necessary to resist evil and to live a wholesome life. Demonic powers are realities with which we must contend daily. They are not little beings in red suits wielding a pitchfork. They are incarnational realities often manifested in ideologies, concepts, principles, organizations, institutions, governments, and even laws. As Eve was thoroughly deceived in the Garden of Eden by the subtlety of the Serpent, our lives are constantly under the threat of the strategies and tactics of the demonic world. Human ability alone is not adequate to overcome these subtle evil forces.

People need a viable Christian force in their lives. In order for religion to be a vital force, it must bring the individual into a genuine relationship with the Holy Spirit. Biblical instructions should not be limited to prohibitions and notifications of the consequences of human failures. People need instructions in righteousness and in the issues of life in order to discern the way of evil and the way of good. This is perhaps what the apostle Paul had in mind when he wrote to Timothy that the word of God is profitable for "doctrine, for reproof, for correction, for instruction in righteousness" (II Tim. 3:16). The emphasis has often been on the use of Scripture for "doctrine," "reproof," and "correction," but there has not been enough focus on the Word for "instruction in righteousness." Instruction is better than correction. And a religious orientation that gives Biblical instructions in how to live a whole life is more profitable than one that simply notifies us of the consequences of failure.

Religion cannot replace the role of parents or family. The family should provide value clarification, character adjustments, and role models, which shape our identity. The family should nurture proper behavior development and emphasize respect for life, law, and order. Christian orientation may determine the foundation of these values, behaviors, and attitudes, but the home is the place of early training.

The Church, universal and local, must be able to discern its mission and the tactics and strategies necessary to accomplish them. It must be able to distinguish between its ministry to the individual and its ministry to the nations of the world. Salvation of the individual may be the center of God's will, but it is not the circumference. Our God is a world being and exhibits concern for the entire created order. The Church, therefore, must be able to properly assess the challenges that exist in the world and then establish the priorities of its involvement. There are vast consequences of unregeneracy that exist in the world such as poverty, ignorance, wars and crimes against humanity: but the Church must understand its jurisdictional authority and clearly discern its battle zones.

If the kingdoms of this world are to become the kingdoms of our God and of His Christ, then the Church must understand the strategies and tactics of the Kingdom of God.

Economic domination, powerful military bases, and technological warfare may be effective strategies, but they are foreign to the methods of advancing the Kingdom of God. The institutional Church is not the only agency to affect change and influence. God works through people in the sphere of existence where He finds them. Therefore, the Church must be able to determine how best to work with other entities such as governments, educational institutions, correctional institutions, financial organizations, and all groups that represent authority and influence in the world. The Church cannot do all things nor can it be all things. Therefore, it must clearly identify its role and mission and the parameters of its involvement in society.

This book will hopefully obligate individuals to begin a quest to broaden their sense of perception in order to discern the options appropriately. Because methods change but principles remain constant, the book's instruction focuses on developing principles as a tool of discernment.

CHAPTER 2

Discernment Defined

Webster's dictionary defines the term "discern" as the ability to detect with the eyes or with other senses than vision in order to identify and to understand differences. The common Biblical recognition of the word "discern" is in its association with "spirit" in I Corinthians 12:10. The apostle Paul lists the "discerning of spirits" (diakrisis pneuma) as one of the gifts of the Holy Spirit that enables a believer to distinguish or judge the nature of the spirit present.

"Spirits" may refer to a wide range of the human, the demonic, and the angelic (Gen. 16:9, 19:1, 31:11; Josh. 5:13-15; Judges 6:22; I Sam. 17:23, 28:7-19; Daniel 10:5-21; Acts 8:5-7,20-24,12:7-10,21-23,13:6-11, 16-19). All human beings are a "house of spirits" (I Corinthians 14:32, 17:16; II Corinthians 2:13). Demons are unclean, evil, and destructive forces (Mark 1:23-25, 9:25; Acts 16:16-18). Angels are "ministering spirits" (Hebrews 1:14; Acts 27:23-24). Hence, discerning of spirits is the ability to distinguish between a whole range of spirits that may be operating in a given space and time. This illumination or distinguishing is possible only by the Holy Spirit operating through the spirit of the individual.

The Apostle Paul concludes the epistle to the Ephesians with an admonition that has served as a foundation for Christian warfare:

> *Finally, my brethren, be strong in the Lord, and in the power of his might. Put on the whole armor of God, that ye may be able to stand against the wiles of the devil. We wrestle not against flesh and blood, but against principalities, against powers, against the rulers of the darkness of this world, against spiritual wickedness in heavenly places. (Ephesians 6:10-12)*

The enemy is clearly identified as not being flesh and blood, but principalities (archai), powers (exousia), against the rulers of the darkness of this world (kosmokratoras), and spiritual wickedness in heavenly places. These opponents are not human; they are superhuman. In Ephesians 2:2 Paul clearly states that individual sins are "blueprinted" not only after the evil social order, but also "according to the prince (archōn) of the power of the air." Wickedness exists external to the individual in the order of society and in the activity of powerful supernatural beings.

To understand the powers that the Apostle Paul is describing, it is important to understand the concept of evil in the Jewish mind. Violence, oppression, and lawlessness were viewed as the consequences of a structure of wickedness, personified by fallen angels (I Enoch 6-11). New Testament writers frequently cited this community in order to give a Biblical account of the social and political situations of their day. The New Testament concept of the world (cosmos) is an effort to show that evil and wickedness did not rest entirely upon the decisions of human beings but may be concealed in the social order and culture. This is not to nullify personal responsibility in the manifestation of evil, but it is a recognition that the oppositions to righteousness are related to "spoiled principalities and powers" (Colossians 2:15).

The New Testament concept of "cosmos" represents humanity seeking to govern itself apart from God. It is humanity with all its devices, schemes, and government seeking to silence the voice of God (Psalms 2; Acts 4). The "cosmos" includes systems of government, property and wealth (I John 3:17), economic relationships (James 2:5; I Corinthians 1:27-28), class and social stratification (Galatians 3:28; Colossians 3:11). The world has its own wisdom (I Corinthians 1:20), values (II Timothy 4:10; I John. 2:15-16), and its own learning (I Corinthians 2:13). So the believer is warned not to be "conformed to this world" that is established on wrong principles (Romans 12:2).

"Powers and principalities" as New Testament realities are described as fallen angels and spirits connected with Satan (Ephesians 2:2; 5:11-12). These "spoiled principalities" are in subjection to Christ (Col. 2:15; I Peter 3:22). They attempt to separate Christians from the love of God in Christ (Romans 8:38-39). The demonic world has authored doctrines that can shipwreck the faith of the believer (I Tim. 4:1). Heretical teachings could overthrow the faith of many (II Tim. 2:15-18). Paul warned the Colossians against a philosophy that sought to nullify the sufficiency of Christ while bringing them into bondage of holy days, self-abasement, worship of angels, and food purity (Colossians 2:8-23). The same Apostle Paul warned the Church at Thessalonica not to be "shaken in mind, or be troubled, neither by spirit, nor by word, nor by letter as from us, as that the day of Christ is at hand" (II

Thessalonians 2:2). The Church at Galatia had been "bewitched" into believing doctrines and practices that were contrary to faith (Gal. 3:1-3). The Apostle John warned the believers of contrary spirits and false prophets that were capable of distorting the faith (I John 4:13).

Whenever demonic forces are at work upon an individual or a group, there are certain characteristics that are prevalent in the attitude and behavior. Some of these characteristics are listed below:

1. A narrowing of the awareness or of the conscious level

There is a decline in the willingness to learn anything new or make necessary changes for the overall benefit of the individual or group. Isolation of the individual or group by a restriction of knowledge of other people, activities, or ideologies is a promotion of ignorance. The Holy Spirit promotes growth and expansion by involvement and a broader awareness of the existence of other people and ideas beyond ourselves.

2. A conscious suppression of creativity and liberty

Growth and maturity is not possible without the freedom of the individual or the group to make their own choices and judgments in order to expand the range of their own initiative. Unnecessary restraints and prohibitions without constructive instruction create a mental dependency and a fear of exploration. Whenever the Spirit of the Lord is at work, there is a liberty and a freedom even in the exchange of ideas and information. Growth is encouraged in an environment that promotes new thoughts and activities without fear.

3. Arrested growth and spiritual immaturity

Excessive authoritarianism and domination prohibit the development of the ability to reason and to make personal decisions and judgments. The Holy Spirit guides and fosters a climate of personal growth by allowing individuals to assume responsibility for their decisions and judgments.

4. Extreme judgment of the beliefs, practices, and attitudes of others.

Constant accusations against others in an effort at self-justification are highly suspicious of demonic activity. This often results in the individual or the group becoming very sectarian and separate from other mainline religious bodies. The final judgment of any individual or group is a divine issue and not limited to human reasoning.

An example of the above criteria occurred when a young woman came into my office suffering from extreme weight loss. She had been fasting for weeks and felt compelled to continue. She had isolated herself from all of her acquaintances. Her performance at work had declined to such a level that she had been placed on probation. When I questioned her about the extensive fasting and behavior at work, she explained her actions as being spiritual and directed by the Holy Spirit. Whenever she attempted to discontinue the fasting or the reading of the Bible during normal office work hours, she experienced great guilt, condemnation, and fear. I informed her that demonic forces motivate people to engage in activities by guilt, fear, and condemnation. There was no Biblical basis for the extremes of her fasting. Furthermore, her reading of the Scriptures during normal working hours was a violation of her employment contract. She would not accept the possibility that the forces influencing her were anything but divine and continued her activities. She was later released from her employment and hospitalized for malnutrition.

Whenever such a departure from orthodox beliefs and practices occur and there is an isolation from the established community of family and friends, our attention should be directed to the sources motivating such behavior. To break ranks with the status quo is not always an admission of demonic intrusion, since every scientific discovery or technological advancement has occurred because of a break with the continuity of the established community; however, condemnation, feelings of extreme guilt, fear and anxiety are not characteristics of divine activity.

The Biblical use of the term "discernment" is in a broader connotation throughout the Scriptures. It means, "to distinguish between person" (Acts 15:9), or to "judge" (I Corinthians 6:5; Matthew 16:3). Discernment includes properly "discriminating the meaning of the bread and the cup of the Lord's Supper" (I Corinthians 11:29,31); and with regard to spiritual utterances in a gathering of believers, it is used in "determining what is of the Holy Spirit" (I Corinthians 14:29). The word "discern" carries the connotation of testing, proving, scrutinizing, approving and disapproving. Its usage seems not to be limited just to the "spirit world," but applies to every dimension of life, which may require identification, approval, or disapproval.

Discernment may involve the scrutinizing of motivations, ethics, and morality as shown in the prayer request of Solomon upon assuming the office of King and his handling of a subsequent case of disputed maternity (I Kings 3:5-10,16-27). In the New Testament when Israel failed to respond appropriately to the visitation of God, Jesus rebuked them sternly for their insensitivity: "Ye hypocrites, ye can discern the face of the sky and of the earth; but how is it ye do not discern this time?" This passage clearly denotes the significance of specific times and seasons and the need to perceive them correctly in order to determine appropriate responses.

Discernment also requires some standard. Whenever appropriate principles or boundaries are established, the process of discernment is facilitated. When Peter came to Antioch, Paul rebuked him because of his partiality in dealing with the Gentiles. When Paul saw that Peter did not walk uprightly according to "the truth of the Gospel," he rebuked Peter openly (Galatians 2:11-21). Here, Paul responded based upon Peter's deviation from the standard of truth. Hence, discernment is also an act of "policing the principles." It is the process of ensuring that behavior, responses and actions are in keeping with some established code.

Discernment may involve the use of the gifts of the Holy Spirit, such as the word of knowledge, word of wisdom, and prophecy. Paul in his epistle to Timothy encourages the young minister to "neglect not the gift that is in thee, which was given thee by prophecy, with the laying on of the hands of the presbytery" (I Timothy 4:14). Here is an example where the revelation gifts of the Holy Spirit are used to ascertain the calling and gifting of a young minister. The Presbytery knew to lay hands on Timothy by a word of knowledge. Prophecy gave divine insight into the will and purpose of God for the young man. A word of wisdom perhaps gave some understanding of the process and future development of the young minister. All of these gifts of the Holy Spirit were working together to identify, affirm, and motivate ministry in the youthful Timothy with the hope that he would be equipped to make sound decisions in the future discharge of his ministry.

It appears from these examples that the term "discernment" is not limited to "spirits," but takes on a broader usage throughout the Scriptures. The term appears to cover the full range of human activities and involvement that require distinguishing, approving, or disapproving.

Discernment

It is this broader usage of the term that we will explore.

CHAPTER 3

Discernment and the Spirit Realm

Are there clear distinctions between evil spirit manifestation, undisciplined behavior, and the ministration of the Holy Spirit? When unusual and destructive behavior is exhibited by a normally calm and disciplined individual, is there evil spirit activity or a momentary loss of control? What is the source of the visions, dreams, and the "inner impressions" that many Christians have reportedly received? A group of young men and women attempted suicide claiming they were under supernatural direction. There have been reports of revivalism with numerous manifestations of people being "slain in the spirit," "barking like a dog," and being overcome with bouts of unusual laughter. Is it God? Is it Satanic? Is it flesh? Let us examine this world of the unseen.

The Scriptures have a lot to say about this spiritual world of angels and demons. Every writer of the New Testament, except the author of Hebrews, mentions demons or evil angels. The first three gospels records 17 references to demons connected with the ministry of Christ. Likewise, in the book of Acts, Luke records 10 references to demonic activity:

1. But Peter said, "Ananias, why hath Satan filled thine heart to lie to the Holy Ghost, and to keep back part of the price of the land"? Acts 5:3

2. There came out a multitude out of the cities round about unto Jerusalem, bringing sick folks, and them which were vexed with unclean spirits: and they were healed everyone. Acts 5:16

3. For unclean spirits, crying with loud voice, came out of many that were possessed with them; and many taken with palsies, and that were lame, were healed. Acts 8:7

4. But there was a certain man called Simon, which before time in the same city used sorcery, and bewitched the people of Samaria, giving out that himself was some great one. Acts 8:9

5. And when they had gone through the isle unto Pathos, they found a certain sorcerer, a false prophet, a Jew, whose name was Barjesus, which was with the deputy of the country, Sergius Paulus, a prudent man; who called for Barnabas and Saul, and desired to hear the word of God. But Elymus the sorcerer (for so is his name by interpretation) withstood them, seeking to turn away the deputy from the faith. Then Saul, who also is called Paul, filled with the Holy Ghost, set his eyes on him, and said, O thou, full of subtlety and all mischief, thou child of the devil, thou enemy of all righteousness, wilt thou not cease to pervert the right way of the Lord? And now, behold, the hand of the Lord is upon thee, and thou shalt be blind not seeing the sun for a season ." And immediately there fell on him a mist and a darkness; and he went about seeking some to lead him by the hand. Acts 13:6-11

6. And it came to pass, as we went to prayer, a certain damsel possessed with a spirit of divination met us, which brought her masters much gain by soothsaying: the same followed Paul and us, and cried, saying, "These men are the servants of the most high God, which shew unto us the way of salvation." And this did she many days. But Paul, being grieved, turned and said to the spirit, "I command thee in the name of Jesus Christ to come out of her." And he came out of her the same hour. Acts 16:16-18

7. So that from his body were brought unto the sick handkerchiefs or aprons, and the diseases departed from them, and the evil spirits went out of them. Then certain of the vagabond Jews, exorcists, took upon them to call over them which had evil spirits the name of the Lord Jesus, saying, "We adjure you by Jesus whom Paul preacheth," and there were seven sons of one Sceva, a Jew, and chief of the priest, which did so. And the evil spirit answered and said, "Jesus I know, and Paul I know; but who are ye?" And the man in whom the evil spirit was leaped on them, and overcame them, and prevailed against them, so that they fled out of that house naked and wounded. Acts 19:12- 17

8. Many used curious arts brought their books together and burned them before the men; and they counted the price of them, and found it fifty thousand pieces of silver. Acts 19:19

9. For a certain man named Demetrius, a silversmith, which made silver shrines for Diana, brought no small gain unto the craftsmen; whom he called together with the workmen of like occupation, and said, "Sirs, ye know that by this craft we have our wealth. Moreover ye see and hear, that not alone at Ephesus, but almost throughout all Asia, this Paul hath persuaded and turned away much people, saying that they be no gods, which are made with hands; so that not only this our craft is in danger to be set at naught; but also that the temple of the great goddess Diana should be despised, and her mag-

nificence should be destroyed, whom all Asia and the world worshippeth. "And when they heard these sayings, they were full of wrath, and cried out, saying, "Great is Diana of the Ephesians." And the whole city was filled with confusion; and having caught Gaius and Aristarchus, men of Macedonia, Paul's companions in travel, they rushed with one accord into the theatre. And when Paul would have entered in unto the people, the disciples suffered him not. And certain of the chief of Asia, which were his friends, sent unto him, desiring him that he would not adventure himself into the theatre. Some therefore cried one thing, and some another; for the assembly was confused and the more part knew not wherefore they were come together. And they drew Alexander out of the multitude, the Jews putting him forward. And Alexander beckoned with the hand, and would have made his defense unto the people. But when they knew that he was a Jew, all with one voice about the space of two hours cried out, "Great is Diana of the Ephesians. "And when the town clerk had appeased the people, he said, "Ye men of Ephesus, what man is there that knoweth not how that the city of the Ephesians is a worshiper of the great goddess Diana, and of the image which fell down from Jupiter? Seeing then that these things cannot be spoken against, ye ought to be quiet, and to do nothing rashly." Acts 19:24-36

10. To open their eyes, and to turn them from darkness to light, and from the power of Satan unto God, that they may receive forgiveness of sins, and inheritance among them which are sanctified by faith that is in me. Acts 20:18

The New Testament also makes references to angels. These immortal and celestial creatures are represented as messengers of God with a knowledge of and an interest in earthly affairs:

1. But of that day and hour knoweth no man, no, not the angels of heaven. (Matthew 24:36)

2. And behold, there talked with him two men, which were Moses and Elias; who appeared in glory, and spake of his decease which he should accomplish at Jerusalem. (Luke 9:31)

3. For when they shall rise from the dead, they neither marry, nor are given in marriage; but are as the angels which are in heaven. (Mark 12:25)

4. I say unto you, that likewise joy shall be in heaven over one sinner that repenteth more than over ninety and nine just persons, which need no repentance. (Luke 15:7)

5. Likewise, I say unto you, there is joy in the presence of the angels of God over one sinner that repenteth. Luke 15:10

6. I charge thee before God, and the Lord Jesus Christ, and the elect angels that thou observe these things without preferring one before another, doing nothing by partiality. I Timothy 5:21

7. Unto whom it was revealed, that not unto themselves but unto us they did minister the things, which are reported unto you by them that have preached the gospel unto you with the Holy Ghost sent down from heaven; which things the angels desire to look into. I Peter 1:1

Angels actively promote divine purposes through their devoutness (Matthew 24:31, 26:53; Acts 7:53; Galatians 3:19). These spirit beings, both angelic and demonic, are intelligent creatures with supernatural powers.

There is no indication that these spiritual beings were mere transitional entities that ceased to be active after the time of Christ and the apostles. The New Testament writers affirm the generational continuation of spiritual activities (I Tim; 2 Thess. 2:1-12; I John 4:1-3). In fact,

a part of the mission of the Church is to make known unto these principalities and powers the "manifold wisdom of God" (Ephesians 3:10).

There is substantial Biblical evidence to indicate that demonic activity influences Christians (Eph. 6:11-18; I Thess. 2:18; I Tim. 3:6-
7,4:1; I Peter 5:6-8; 2 Peter 2:1-22). Whether the influence is indirect
(as through deceptive teachers, prophets, and false doctrines), or direct
(as through sickness, psychological disorders, and possession), it does
exist. The first tendency is to dismiss the existence of demonic oppression. This attitude is the result of an effort to relegate all human
dysfunction to scientific explanation. And if demonic forces are only
historic entities out of the pages of the gospels and the apostolic jour-
nals, then the only plausible explanation for diseases and psychological
disorders must be scientific and the treatment must be medical. The
second tendency is to dismiss the scientific and to over-emphasize the
spiritual. This approach generally subordinates medical intervention
to deliverance. It does not take into consideration the complexity of
the human ego, personality or the origin and progression of disease.

Neither of the above tendencies alone takes into consideration the
physical, psychological, spiritual, nor genetic factors that must be evaluated in the diagnosis and treatment of the human problems we face
daily. A better approach would be to acknowledge the possibility of a
plurality of causes in reference to human maladies. Such an approach
would necessitate a union between faith and medicine. The spiritual
counselor and the scientist must be considered a team organized to
diagnose the distinction between the physical and the spiritual. This
would mandate that training curriculum for counselors include courses in demonology, psychology, and medicine in order to broaden the
student's perception of pastoral care. It would also be necessary for
medical personnel to have a knowledge of demonology.

The critical issue is the identification of the causes of the problems. Demonization is not caused by a chemical imbalance in the brain that may be aggravated by circumstances, which lead to abnormal emotions, behavior, and thoughts. Such chemical imbalances are generally relieved by the administration of the proper medication. In demonization, the personality of the individual is replaced by the personality of the spirit power. The thought process and behavior of the individual is commonly affected. The physical body can be affected with sicknesses and deformities.[1]

An examination of the Scriptures confirms most of the symptoms listed above. The woman with a physical infirmity that caused her to be bowed down was described as having a spirit of infirmity (Luke 13:11-13). The demoniac described in Mark 5 exhibited symptoms affecting his personality and physical body:

1. Exceptional physical strength (v.3-4)
2. Behavioral manifestation (v. 5)
3. Hyper-religious activities and schizophrenic behavior causing him to worship Jesus in one moment and recoil in fear the next moment (v.6-7)
4. Possession of psychic powers that enabled him to know the identity of Jesus without being informed (v.7)
5. Change of voice (v. 7-9)
6. Passing of the spirits from the man to the swine (v.12-13)

The symptoms ascribed to the demoniac in Mark 5 must be added to other symptoms of dumbness (Luke 11:14), blindness (Matthew 12:22), and seizures (Luke 9:38-42). There are also psychic activities associated with demonic powers that were demonstrated by Simon, the magician who bewitched the people (Acts 8:9-10) and the false prophet, Barjesus (Acts 13:6-11).

Dr. Kurt Koch, in his book "Occult Bondage and Deliverance," makes reference to the work of German psychiatrist Alfred Lechler in which symptoms of demonization are described: violence and cursing, rebellion against God, excessive sexual or sensual desires, disdain of spiritual things, excessive lying and impure thoughts, restlessness and depression, resistance to Christian counselor, inability to write or pronounce the name of Jesus, seizures or bouts of unconsciousness, inability to renounce the works of the devil, excessive physical strength and speaking in unlearned languages.[2] It appears that some of the symptoms of demonization overlap with similar signs of psychological disorders. A tentative diagnosis of demonization would depend upon the prevalence and the grouping of these symptoms.

Whenever there are symptoms that suggest demonic intrusion, there should be an investigation of the history of any psychological, physical or spiritual disorders and treatments. Any spiritism, witchcraft, Satan worship, and drugs should be noted since these provide an open door for demonization.[3] Any ancestral involvement of the individual's family in the occult or other demonic activities should be noted. If there has been any involvement of the individual with any medium, healer or magic for the transference of any powers or gifts, it should be noted. Unger supports such a conclusion:

"In the great majority of cases, possession is doubtless to be traced to yielding voluntarily to temptation and to sin, initially weakening of the human will, so that it is rendered susceptible to complete or partial eclipse and subjugation by the possessing spirit."[4]

Ensign and Howe support such claims with the following statement:

"The usual cause of demonic control over some area (and usually it is only a part of a person's life that is controlled) of personality, will, or body stems from that person's involvement in satanic-occult activities before he became a Christian."[5]

Let's focus a moment on the demonic portion of the spirit realm. Demonic spirits, as an organized group, are capable of devising strategies and schemes (II Corinthians 2:11; Ephesians 6:11-12); controlling human beings (Ephesians 2:1-2); 2nd influencing world government and the direction of history (Dan. 10:13, 20; John 12:31; 1 John 4:1,5; Ephesians 6: 1-12). They can produce the miraculous and generate "power and signs and lying wonders" (2 Thessalonians 2:9). Although God limits these creatures in time, space, power, and knowledge, the deception and power that they generate can be effective. For example:

1. Demons promote evil activities through their control of individuals (Ephesians 2:1-2), institutions (I Corinthians 2:8), and the entire created order (John 12:31; Ephesians 6:11-12; II Thessalonians 2:8-19).

2. Demons oppose Divine purposes (Matthew 16:22- 23; II Thessalonians 2:3-4; I Timothy 4:1-5; I John 4:1-4 3).

3. Demons war with believers and seek to oppose the spread of the Gospel (Luke 8:12; I Corinthians 4:3, 7:2,5; II Corinthians 4:3-4; Ephesians 6:12).

4. Demons seek to corrupt the Church through false doctrine and deception (Galatians 3:1-3; I Timothy 4:1-5; II Corinthians 11:13-15; I John 4:1-4; Colossians 2:18-23).

5. Demons promote division and strife, and they take advan-

tage of the weaknesses of believers (I Corinthians 7:5; II Corinthians 2:10-11; Acts 5:3; Ephesians 4:26-27; I John 2:15-16, 5:19; I Peter 5:6-10).

6. Demons can cause sickness, disease, and mental illnesses (Matthew 9:32-33, 12:22,17:14-18).

Although these demonic forces are powerful and deceptive, they are in subjection to the power of God. The evidence of the Kingdom of God was the exhibited power of the Lord Jesus over demons: "If I cast out demons by the Spirit of God, then the Kingdom of God has come upon you" (Matthew 12:28). Paul describes the triumph of Jesus over all evil as "having spoiled principalities and powers; he made a show of them openly, triumphing over them in it" (Colossians 2:15). Let it clearly be established that in this brief study of the spirit world that there remains the triumphant Christ and the power of God. However, disorders due to chemical imbalances or pathological diseases will not respond to deliverance. They are, however, all within the range of correction through faith and prayer (James 5:14-16). Demonic affliction will respond to the name of Jesus and confrontation. The critical issue is to confirm the diagnosis and provide the appropriate ministry.

Before closing out this section, let us deal with a critical area of discerning the difference between psychic phenomena and Pentecostal power. We have established the fact that the spiritual world includes angels, demons, powers, principalities, thrones, dominions, and rulers of darkness. This world of spirit beings has citizens of "light" and "darkness," and therefore is capable of doing good and evil. As human beings, we learn from our sensory organs of sight, sound, touch, smell, and taste. Our senses allow us to transmit and receive information about the world. However, human beings have the ability to receive information without using the "normal" channels of the senses and the nervous system. This ability enables them to make contact with a non-physical world of spirit beings that cannot be observed by the senses.

Christians, especially among Pentecostals, have known the power of the Holy Ghost as the communicator of divine wisdom and knowledge (John 14:26, 16:13-15). But they have also recognized that there are such phenomena as astrology, fortune-telling, witchcraft, sorcery, and ESP that occasionally provide knowledge and revelation. These spiritual alternatives are considered to come directly from satanic powers and to be wicked. There is a very fine line of demarcation between extrasensory perception and Pentecostal power. The accuracy of a diviner or a fortuneteller is not validation of a divine origin.

The witch of Endor was proficient in calling forth a familiar spirit that accurately predicted the death of Saul (I Samuel 21:19). Elymus, a sorcerer and a false prophet, influenced those with whom he came in contact through divination and the practice of magical arts (Arts 13:6-12). The young girl who followed after Paul and Silas, declaring that they were servants of God, was accurate in her assessment of them (Acts 16:16-19). She was, however, a fortuneteller and relied upon the power of the spirit of darkness and not the Holy Ghost. Paul was grieved in his spirit and exorcised the demon out of the woman. This was the gift of discerning of spirits in operation, enabling the Apostle Paul to determine this demonic activity.

There are times when mediums and diviners are not obvious in their dress or mannerisms. Sometimes they may operate within the realm of what we call orthodox Christian circles. Just because activities occur within the four walls of the assembled Church does not validate their origin as divine. There are three factors that may contribute to the differentiation between the demonic and the divine. These include the source of the information, the motive for the desire of the power, and the intended purpose of the power.

Let us deal first with the intended purpose of the power. Demonic power promotes bondage, stifles creativity, closes channels of communication, and fosters long-range dependency that negates growth and maturity. Demonic forces promote hate, schism, and distinctions based upon sex, race, age, and socioeconomic status. The ultimate purpose of demonic activity is encapsulated in Jesus' rebuke of the Pharisees and scribes: "Woe unto you, scribes and Pharisees, hypocrites! For ye compass sea and land to make one proselyte and when he is made, ye make him twofold more the child of hell than yourselves" (Matthew 23:15). Here, sincere religious activity ensnared the soul of the convert and diverted the individual from the power of God. Elymas the sorcerer used his power for the same purpose of closing off channels of communication between the deputy and Paul (Acts 13:6-8). In both of these instances, the agents were sincere, but sincerity is not a criterion for truth. The litmus test for truth is its fruit. In both of these instances, the intended purpose of the power was to separate the individual from the power or resource of God. Therefore, the ultimate intention was destruction.

The motive for the desire of the power is a key factor. This is difficult to ascertain, but ultimately, it is the fruit that uncovers the motivation. Is the motive to dominate and control others or to possess wealth and authority? Simon the sorcerer desired the power of the Holy Ghost for the above-mentioned reasons (Acts 8:18-19). The proper motive for power is to serve and not to control or gain wealth (I Corinthians 10:1). Jesus declared to His disciples that the desire for greatness and power should be for the purpose of service (Matthew

23:1). Paul admonished the Corinthians when he expressed the proper motive for his power: "Therefore, I write these things being absent lest being present I should use sharpness, according the power which the Lord hath given me to edification, not to destruction" (II Corinthians 13:10). Christianity seems to be in tune with God's power as an agent of His will. It seeks to help people participate more in the life of God, in love, fellowship, growth, and creativity. Any motivation that takes away the personal initiative and guidance of the individual should be suspect.

The source of the power is the most critical issue. Is it Divine or demonic? Jesus declared that when the Holy Ghost came to the earth, He would exhibit certain behavioral traits: "however, when He, the Spirit of truth, is come, he will guide you into all truth; for He shall not speak of himself; but whatsoever He shall hear, that shall He speak; and He will show you things to come. He shall glorify me..." (John 16:13-14). Jesus said that the executive agent of the Trinity, the Holy Ghost, will not act on His own, nor will He glorify Himself. He will speak by commission and will magnify the ministry of Jesus. The ministry of the Holy Ghost will be in agreement with some established norm, the Word. There will be an interdependency and submissiveness about His ministry. He will ultimately enlist people into the army of God because that is a fruit of truth. If the Spirit of God is working in an individual or a group, there must be similar behavioral traits because of His incarnate presence. There will be an interdependency and submissiveness about the nature of their work. The incarnate ministry of the Holy Ghost will not breed confusion, contention, schism, jealousy, domination, or evil fruit.

Whenever evil forces are at work in an individual or a group, there are efforts to dominate or exert power over others. Disunity is common but not always prominent. Opportunities are given on the basis of sex, age, race, and socioeconomic status. Demonic powers engender bondage and narrow the circumference of perception. People are forced to remain within their group or limited circle and are not allowed to interact with a broader populace. Evil activity stifles creativity by resisting change or new ideas or concepts. The demonic nurtures longstanding dependency and addiction, which promotes immaturity. It causes people to become dependent upon others rather than causing them to become responsible for themselves or their own decisions.

These traits are common in cult groups where one or more personalities dominate a whole group through coercion or even force. Individuals of the groups conform to the values and behavior of the dominant groups out of fear of rejection, humiliation, or even physical force. Members of the groups are encouraged to relinquish all of their rights to self-determination. Individual decisions and personal initiatives are viewed as antagonistic to the integrity of the group and, therefore, placed in the hands of a dominant personality. Members of the group are encouraged to sever all relationships with families or friends that are antagonistic to the group.

Whenever the Holy Ghost is at work in an individual or a group, there is an environment that fosters creativity, freedom, and open and honest exchange. There are improved personal relationships rather than unfair distinctions based upon race, age, or socioeconomic status. People are pressed to mature and become responsible in their relations with God and with others. Unity is promoted by broadening the awareness of the existence of other people who may be different. Whenever the Holy Ghost is at work, there is an environment of love and freedom rather than fear and reprisals.

In conclusion to this section, it is necessary that we be aware of the spiritual world and its influences. We must be able recognize possible causes, symptoms and influences of spiritual intrusion. We must be able to discern the work of the spirit world in practices, doctrines, and traditions; and finally be able to discern when to apply the power of God, faith, medicine, and counsel in order to bring wholeness.

Discussion:

1. Explore other examples of the spirit world.

2. Explain some of the characteristics that demonstrate the activity of the Holy Ghost at work among an individual or a group.

3. Explain some of the characteristics prevalent when demonic powers are at work in an individual or a group.

4. Discuss the characteristics of demons at work in practices, doctrines, traditions and behavior.

5. Discuss some of the ways in which faith, prayer and medical science can work together to bring deliverance and wholeness from chemical and pathological diseases.

6. Discuss how the power of the Holy Ghost is like/unlike the psychic phenomena.

7. List different examples of human afflictions and categorize the symptoms and cures for demonic possession, chemical addiction, chemical imbalances, and pathological diseases.

Notes

[1]William M. Alexander, *Demonology in the New Testament* (Edinburg T. & T. Clark, 1902) pp. 147-173

[2]Kurt Koch, *Occult Bondage and Deliverance* (Grand Rapids: Krege 1, 1970) pp. 136-153)

[3]C. Fred Dickason, *Demon Possession and the Christian* (Westchest ILL; Crossway Book, 1987), p. 163

[4]Merrill F. Unger, *Biblical Demonology* (Wheaton, 111; Scripture Pre: s, 1957) p.95

[5]Grayson H. Ensign and Edward Howe, *Bothered? Bewildered? Bewitched?* (Cincinnati: Recovery, 1984), pp. 150-151

CHAPTER 4

Discernment and the Natural Realm

I t is important to acknowledge the presence and influence of the demonic realm. It is equally important to recognize those influ- ences that are not demonic but are, nevertheless, in opposition to the rule and reign of Christ. There are ideologies, concepts, and in- fluences that we "fall under" which advance the work of the demonic realm. Why should demons exert energy when these "hidden persuad- ers" effectively handicap us?

I was conducting a class on the numerous factors affecting our daily decisions and judgments. It was an effort to identify the external in- fluences of the media and marketing upon the values, choices, and be- havior of the general public. We addressed symbols and signs and the manipulation of the nonverbal environment as a propaganda tool. We explored media bias in selection of stories and the presentation or the omission of critical data in articles and news reports. The manipulation of the nonverbal environment of signs and symbols was shown to exert a significant influence upon public judgment and values. Signs and symbols deal with the language of the unconscious, and elicit feelings, emotions, and thoughts. The significance of symbols and signs rests in their inherent power to speak beyond themselves. For example, the strategic placement and the omission of artistic signs and symbols, as in the case of Biblical nativity scenes on government property, communicates an influential message.

The Lord Jesus warned his disciples to be "wise as serpents" (Matt. 10:6). Gullibility is not a valuable asset for anyone, especially a Christian. The Biblical admonition is to "prove all things and hold fast to that which is good."[1] However, excessive skepticism can be contrary to a life of faith. Uncontrolled doubt and suspicions can negatively affect the will to believe. Yet, there is a need, I believe, to consider the dynamics of the powerful force field of knowledge and information that has invaded our environment. Asking questions and seeking clarity are activities on the road to discovering wisdom and knowledge.

There are several philosophical concepts that exert an influence upon our rational judgment, behavior, and attitude. Human beings are complex entities, for they are spiritual, physical, and psychological. Therefore, in this section we shall address several concepts: antinomianism, procession, intentionalism, utilitarianism, and skepticism.

Antinomianism. The term "antinomianism" literally means "against the law." It is the belief that one can live outside the boundaries of regulations and laws of society. From a theological perspective, antinomianism is the belief that faith alone, not moral law, is necessary for salvation. The antinomian is one who attempts to live above any law or social restrictions because of some faith, grace, or knowledge that grants salvation.

Christianity has always recognized that justification by faith does not deny the restraints of moral law.[2] The Corinthian epistle is a classic example of the Apostle Paul's efforts to maintain a proper tension between faith and moral law in the lives of the people. The antinomian is one who attempts to justify any moral perversion by pleading the power of faith alone. A proper tension must exist between the instructive value of Biblically revealed moral law and the power of faith in the life of the believer. Without some universal guidelines and landmarks to direct the ethical and moral course, then every person is left to do that which seems right in his/her own sight. Judges 21:25 reflects such a state: "In those days there was no king in Israel; every man did that which was right in his own eyes." The logical progression of such thinking is "situational ethics" in which judgment is made from the "force of the moment" rather than from the gravitational influence of a historic law. I realize the extreme of legalism in the opposite direction where a law never takes in consideration the transcending factors or circumstances. But the antinomian does not recognize any historic continuum; and consequently, human behavior, values, and judgment, are reduced to the level of a lower animal that lives by instinct alone.

During a time of ministry in a local Church, I allowed a time for questions and answers after my time of teaching. A young man asked me if it were acceptable to have a "spiritual wife" in addition to his wife. He gave reference to a verse in I Corinthians 9:1-5 in which Paul is addressing his detractors. "Am I not an apostle? Am I not free? Have I not seen Jesus Christ our Lord? Are not ye my work in the Lord? If I be not an apostle unto others, yet doubtless I am to you; for the seal of mine apostleship are ye in the Lord. Mine answer to them that do examine me is this, have we not power to eat and to drink? Have we not power to lead about a sister, a wife, as well as other apostles, and as the brethren of the Lord, Cephas?" He felt that the reference to a "sister" gave license to the concept of "spiritual wife." A "spiritual wife," in his understanding, was a very special woman who would meet the needs that his own wife was not fulfilling. The only exception was sexual intimacy. I explained that the scripture reference had no connection to such a concept and that marriage provided absolute boundaries regarding the conduct and behavior of the husband and the wife. And to suggest that this passage gave license to pursue a social relationship outside of the boundaries of marriage for the purpose of fulfilling emotional needs not being addressed in the marriage was not justified by faith nor any "situation ethics." This represented a classic example of antinomianism in which the restraints of moral law are exceeded by an alleged permission to live beyond such boundaries.

Proeessionism. The early Greek philosophers took for granted that things change.[3] They saw change all about them and did not recognize it as a problem. Water changed into ice or ice to steam, air became wind; numbers became things; motion was in everything producing these changes.

The universe, then, is ruled by "conflict." Just as in music harmony results from the combination of low and high notes. In the universe harmony results from the combination of opposites, good and evil.[4] The moment a thing is made, conflict begins to break it up. If this kind of reasoning is expanded to the realm of law, it becomes very clear that there can be no abiding landmarks. Since everything is changing and the absolute becomes relative, what was wrong today comes right tomorrow.

Such a view eliminates any concept of transcendence. It is understandable that knowledge and technology are progressive. The automobile, the train, and the airplane have replaced the horse and buggy.

Yet, outside the realm of science and technology, are there truths and principles that are applicable to every generation? Should concepts of human worth, respect for life, and individual freedom possess a place of permanent residence in the laws of every evolving generation? If not, then the possibility of euthanasia, fratricide, genocide, and ultimately deicide can become moral considerations in the evolving culture. In fact, we struggle with these ideas even now in the moral evolution of our nation.

Intentionalism. This concept argues that an act is right if it is done with the good intentions and wrong if done with bad intentions.[5] The act is not viewed as right or wrong, just the motive or intent. Saul of Tarsus had good intentions of stamping out the early phases of Christianity (Acts 26). According to intentionalism, his actions were good because his intentions were good. The same argument could be applied to Hitler and every political assassin who had good intentions. Intentionalism removes any ethics or morality since the rightness or wrongness is solely based on the intent of the individual.

Skepticism. Faith is described as a firm belief in something for which there may not be a tangible or visible proof. Skepticism is a persistent doubting or a state of disbelief. It is a state of suspended judgment precipitated by a persistent rational and critical examination of everything.[6] From an ethical standpoint, the skeptic insists that every issue has two sides; and therefore, nothing should ever be considered absolute right or wrong.[7] A New Testament admonition is to "prove all things and hold fast to that which is good" (I Thess. 5:21). The prophet Malachi challenged Israel to put God to the test (Malachi 3:10). Truth is discovered by searching, challenging, and discerning the subject in question. The skeptic constantly "halts between two opinions" (I Kings 18:21) without bringing a finality to the search.

Paul speaks of individuals who are "ever learning and never able to come to the knowledge of the truth" (II Timothy 3:7). This is the description of the skeptic who is constantly imprisoned somewhere between the beginning and the ending of the search. Suspicion and doubt prevents the skeptic from coming to some finality in judgment.

All of these concepts are capable of influencing doctrines and ideologies, which ultimately become the undisputed basis for some ethical or theological decisions and judgments. Good and evil can be expressed in beliefs and doctrines (I Tim. 4:1-3). Therefore, spiritual warfare is not "beating the air with our fist, but taking a vigilant stand against the subtle influences on our minds, whether they be doctrinal or philosophical.

PREJUDICE

What motivates disunity and strife between people who are different racially, culturally, or nationally? What accounts for the gender crisis and the continuous struggle of women to achieve proper status with men? Is there the involvement of the spirit world, or should we look for answers in other places? These are perhaps significant questions in light of the rising tide of human disorientation and the numerous efforts of social reconciliation that are occurring worldwide. In this section we will discuss some of the causes and possible solutions.

GENERATIONAL PREJUDICE

The way we perceive people who are different from ourselves may not always be based upon our own evaluation, but upon generations of beliefs, values, and ideologies that have somehow been passed on to us through family, friends, intellectuals, politicians, and even religious leaders. It is unlikely that many of the presuppositions concerning these "different people" were ever really questioned. Because the source of information was trusted, it is probable that the information was not critically examined. For example, racial prejudice may be a social attitude supported by generational beliefs that certain peoples are "inferior" or that they are a "lower form of creation." Another example is the social stigma attached to gender. The book of Genesis has been used to support the theory that women are to be in subjection to men because of a creational decree by God. The evidence to support such a claim is based upon the order of creation, the satanic deception, and the curse of God supposedly placed upon the woman in the beginning (Genesis 1-3). Although such a theory has no sound biblical support, it has been transmitted from generation to generation as sound Biblical reasoning for the subjugation of women in their homes, in churches, and in society. A brief review of the Genesis story does not place any status on the order of creation since the animals, a lower species were created before all humanity (Genesis 1:1,2,10,20-27).

If the order of creation carried with it a status, then the earth and creatures would have dominion over humanity. The woman was not created from the "rib" of the man, a theory which is used to subordinate the role of women to men (Gene 2:22). The word "rib" is taken from the Hebrew word *tsela*, which also means "side" or "side chamber." Eve was not an evil creature who collaborated with the serpent to deceive Adam. Both Adam and Eve were sinless creatures before the fall. The Genesis story clearly states that Eve was deceived or thoroughly convinced to believe a lie (Genesis 3:1-12). The woman was not cursed according to some historical misunderstandings. Only the serpent and the ground were cursed (Genesis 3:14-19). In fact a covenantal decree by God regarding the seed of the woman foretold the demise of Satan (Genesis 3:15).

The same tendencies are found in the association of certain human characteristics with sex. The genes that determine physical distinctions between men and women have no association with the intellectual or the psychological traits. The roles assigned to women and the privileges denied them cannot be justified by any sexual genetic differences. The same applies to race. No one sex or race is more endowed or gifted than another because of some "gene factor." There are indeed physical differences between the sexes and the races. However, the physical differences are most often used as the significant criteria in awarding or denying privileges and rights.

Race has been a source of extreme confusion. The confusion rests in the failure to recognize the difference between race and ethnic group. All too often we associate differences in customs, values, intellectual abilities, and behavior to race. Hence, we erroneously conclude that all Blacks have the same values, opinions, and abilities. The same conclusion is drawn for Caucasians, Asians, Indians, and Asians. Very little consideration is given to environmental and social conditioning. When we confuse the existing differences between people because of racial and ethnic traits, we are confusing what is gained through learning from what is given by nature. What is given by heredity is more difficult to change than that which is a product of learning or environmental conditioning.

Most human characteristics that are usually ascribed to race are actually the products of cultural and environmental influences and should be regarded as ethnic and not racial. An ethnic trait is acquired. And there are some human characteristic dominant in every ethnic group that are a consequence of conditioning and acquired behavior. Such differences may include language, food, child rearing, music, hairstyles, gestures, funeral rites, marriage ceremonies, religious customs, occupations, and clothing preferences. The key point to remember is that these outward traits are ethnic and not racial. And because they are acquired from the culture, they are not consistently present in the racial group. Hence, the same values and preferences in music, food, clothing, and occupations may be shared with members of different racial groups.

ENVIRONMENTAL PREJUDICE

The influence of environmental factors may contribute significantly to certain attitudes and beliefs concerning race and gender. Many times our responses to others are but minor images of what we see around us. All groups or cultures develop a way of living within the restraints of certain codes, beliefs, and standards. Such groups may even have a common enemy. Individual members of the group may not even question the prevalent attitudes and behaviors that surround them. They may even emulate some of the attitudes and behaviors because of the social pressures to conform and the need to be accepted by the dominant group. The enemies of the groups may then become the enemies of the individual. The nation of Israel during Old Testament times is a classic example of such a group that lived within the constraints of Divine laws.

All individuals do not conform to the norms, values, or behavior of the community in which they reside. Some individuals are non-conformists. However, the pressures of the environmental factors can exert tremendous influences on the attitude and behavior of the individual. For example, the religious environment demonstrates this point. All great religions adhere to what they describe as absolute and final truths. Each group insists that its members practice its creeds and doctrines. Consequently, members who do not adhere to these creeds and doctrines will find themselves in disagreement with the common group. Historic Judaism and Christianity were at extreme odds because of such differences. Each group possessed creeds and doctrines that placed them in conflict with one another. Christians were martyrs because of their convictions and were viewed as the common enemy of Judaism.

Within the Christian environment, then, the seeds for prejudice are sown. This occurs, in my judgment, because the Christian Church and its various denominations stand for more than faith. Denominational Christianity has become a representation of the cultural traditions and norms of a group. For example, as a young boy growing up in a rural Methodist Church, I can remember many cultural traditions of the people that were fostered in the Church. The annual revivals and family reunions with all of the celebrations and food were first cultural traditions that were later incorporated into the traditions of the Church. A neighboring Pentecostal Church had become a subculture with its emphasis on dress codes and social behaviors. Its members were prohibited from attending sports activities or movie theaters. The women in particular did not wear cosmetics. Anyone who did not conform to the codes and doctrines of that cultural environment were not warmly accepted. In both the Methodist and the Pentecostal Churches in my neighborhood, there were traditions and doctrines that tended to cause tensions between people. And in many instances, individuals who were outside the boundaries of those traditions and doctrines were excluded from fellowship.

During my childhood days in the south, Blacks and Whites did not attend the same Churches together. Segregation was rampant, and religion was contaminated with racial prejudice. The Churches seemed to be a reflection of the status quo of race relations in the communities rather than being a mixed racial Christian community. This is not to say that bigotry was exclusively religious. However, religion became a representation of the values and altitudes of an ethnic and a racial group, and religion fostered an environment where prejudice thrived and was justified.

The public media and advertisement may also influence our concepts regarding race, culture, gender, and even age. However, how a certain group is portrayed by the moviemakers and the advertising media can greatly influence the individual's concentration of the poor, rich, young, old, male, female, and even ethnic or racial group. Standards presented to us by the advertising media causes us to desire luxury, status, and youthfulness. Such influences can create disdain for the poor, racial groups, and even the elderly. Some of the roles played by minorities in movies and television have contributed to stereotypes of such groups. Some of the supporting roles played by Asians, Blacks, and Hispanics during the 1950s and the 1960s did influence public attitudes and beliefs concerning these groups.

We have a tendency to make generalizations based upon little factual evidence. For example, the belief that moral trails, mental capacities, and physical aptitude are linked to skin color is a broad generalization. The belief that a person's character is associated with their physical appearance is stereotypical. The idea that women are weak, incapable of governing others is rooted in an erroneous belief that associate mental capabilities and performance levels with gender. The belief that Blacks are "shiftless" and that Hispanics are "lazy" is predicated up some of the stereotypical images presented of Blacks and Hispanics in the motion picture industry.

Our experiences with people who are different than ourselves can greatly influence our perception of an entire group. While completing my dental residency in Boston, I had the opportunity of meeting with a group of my peers. They represented different racial and ethnic groupings. One member of the group expressed to me how he had hated all Americans because of his childhood experiences during the war. He had formed a general hatred of all members of a group because of his experiences with a few members of that group. Group stereotyping is the result of making broad categorization of racial and ethnic groupings without evaluating individual members of the group.

It has been my experience that people are not the same in their values, behavior, and attitudes just because they belong to a certain racial group. A pastor was discussing with me plans for a transcultural ministry. He believed that Blacks were emotional and preferred Gospel music and "fiery preaching," while Whites were more emotionally controlled and expressed a preference for hymns, classical music, and teaching. So he planned to invite some choirs and preachers who could probably reach the Blacks and Whites respectively. Although such a plan seemed to be a practical approach to attracting different ethnic and racial groups, its logic was faulty. Furthermore, such thinking perpetuates some of the unfortunate stereotypes that have plagued society and the Church for decades. Musical preferences and other social interests are neither genetic nor restricted to a certain racial group. They are a matter of individual preference and environmental conditioning. Therefore, any program is scheduled for future difficulty if it attempts to develop a transcultural ministry based upon the belief that individual members of a racial group have the same values, interests, and preferences.

A transcultural ministry must be based upon the truth that God has made all Christians of one blood through Jesus Christ. If there are any ethnic preferences in music or ministry due to cultural conditioning, they must be ultimately subordinated to the transcultural preferences that do not perpetuate polarizations of the group. That is, rather than fostering concepts of Black White, Hispanic, or Asian interests, there should be strategies for the development of true Christian interests. Of course, this demands an identification of the true Christian preferences in music and ministry.

The critical conclusion to be drawn is that prejudice is faulty judgments, irrational behavior, and biased attitudes. The participation of the spirit world cannot be ruled out. However, there are other factors to be considered. And if we are to guard against the detrimental influences of this natural realm, there are a few guidelines to follow:

1. Concepts or philosophies that direct behavior or attitudes away from Biblically based ethics and morality should questioned.

2. Traditions that foster a separation of ethnic or racial groups should be challenged.

3. Absolute rules regarding the value of life, respect for others, and freedom of the individual should not be suspended because of circumstances or events or other changing factors without a multitude of counsel and extensive discussion concerning the consequences of such changes.

4. Guard against general categorization of individual or groups based upon sex, age, race, or any natural distinctions without proper consideration of the individual or the group.

5. Be aware of the cultural and environmental influences that shape your personal relationship with people who are different from yourself.

Let us constantly be aware of our environment and all of its potential influences upon our attitude and behavior. But let us also be aware of the ultimate power of God's perfecting work of Christ in us and our own personal responsibility to renew our minds through the knowledge of what it means to be true a Christian.

Notes

[1]Peter A. Angeles, *Dictionary of Philosophy* (New York, New York: Harper Perennial, 1991), p.13.

[2]Carl F. H. Henry, *Christian Personal Ethics* (Grand Rapids: Michigan: Wm. B. Eerdmans Publishing Co., 1957), p.350

[3]S.E Frost, Jr. , *Basic Teachings of the Great Philosophers* (New York: Doubleday, 1962),p.81-87

[4]Ibid.

[5]Norman L. Geisler, *Christian Ethics: Options and Issues* (Grand Rapils, Michigan: Baker Book House, 1990), p.29

[6]Angeles, op. Cit. P.258

[7]ILK. Harrison, ed., *Encyclopedia of Biblical and Christian Ethics* (Nashville, Tennessee: Thomas Nelson Publishers, 1987), p.385

CHAPTER 5

Discernment and Prophecy

There is no topic of Biblical research that has evoked as much discussion as that of prophecy. As we begin this study, let it be said that God alone can foreknow and foretell the future, and He has chosen to confine His foretelling to the Scriptures and the Holy Spirit. The power of God to declare a thing shall come to pass long before it is in existence, and to bring it to pass, is the expression of His sovereignty. The Scriptures give explicit statements that God gave prophetic decrees:

> *I am God, and there is none else; I am God, and there is none like me; Declaring the end from the beginning, and from ancient times things that are not yet done; saying, My counsel shall stand, and l will do all my pleasure.*
> *(Isaiah 46:9-10)*

The right and power of God alone to forecast and fulfill prophecy is recorded by other writers. Moses outlined the test of a prophet's authenticity (Deuteronomy 18:20-22). Jeremiah called on prophets to produce the validation of their prophecies (Jeremiah 28:7-17). All Scripture is given by inspiration of God including its prophetic element (II Timothy 3:16). Holy men of God, moved or carried along by the Holy Ghost, were the messengers and channels of God's prophetic purposes (II Peter 1:21).

One-fourth of the Bible is related to predictive prophecy, or predictions, which at the time of their utterance were still future. So, in this section we will seek to understand some of the principles governing prophets and prophecy in an effort to understand the historic and the contemporary use of this channel of Divine communication.

Let us begin with the basic question of definition: What is a prophet? The Hebrew word for prophet means to "bubble" or "gush" as a description of the frenzied manner of speech of the prophets. The word *nabi* means "to call" or "name" or "announce." Hence the prophet was an "announcer" or "herald" of divine information. Theophile Meek says the verb should be linked to the Akkadian *nabu*, meaning in its active voice "to speak," thus giving the idea, "speaker."[1] William R Albright says that since the nabu is commonly used in the passive voice, it gives the meaning of "one spoken to" or "called,"[2] The Greek word for prophet means to "speak forth" or "fore-tell." It indicates one who speaks forth a message of present or future events. A prophet was a forth-teller and a fore-teller of messages, which were for his day and beyond.

There is a sense in which Old Testament prophets were "Messianic predictors" and the New Testament prophets and apostles were "Messianic clarifiers." The Old Testament prophets foretold some future events concerning the redemptive work of Christ Jesus without a clear understanding of what they were speaking. The apostle Peter addresses this lack of comprehension of the Old Testament prophets:

> *Receiving the end of your faith, even the salvation of your souls. Of which salvation the prophets have inquired and searched, who prophesied of the grace that should come unto you; searching what or what manner of time the Spirit of Christ which was in them did signify, when it testified beforehand the suffering of Christ, and the glory that should follow. (I Peter 1:9-l 1)*

The New Testament prophets and apostles were given clarification of predictions made by their predecessors. The apostle Paul writes in the Ephesian epistle:

> *For this cause I, Paul, the prisoner of Jesus Christ for you Gentiles, if ye have heard of the dispensation of the grace of God "which is given to me to you-ward; how that by revelation he made known unto me the mystery; (as I wrote afore in few words, whereby, when ye read, ye may understand my knowledge in the mystery of Christ) which in other ages was not made known unto the sons of men, as it is now revealed unto his holy apostles and prophets by the Spirit: That the Gentiles should be fellow-heirs, and of the same body and partakers of his promise in Christ by the gospel. (Ephesians 3:1-6)*

Paul explains a progressive and selective character of prophetic revelation. What the Old Testament prophets may have declared without total understanding, the New Testament apostles and prophets, by the Spirit, comprehended the significance and the application. On the day of Pentecost, Peter cites a prophecy of Joel 2:28-32 and declares its meaning and fulfillment (Acts 2:14-21). It is in this sense that what at times may have been predicted by earlier prophets without total understanding was clarified by later apostles and prophets.

Prophets were preachers, or messengers of God. John the Baptist, premier among the prophets, proclaimed, "Repent ye; for the kingdom of heaven is at hand" (Matthew 3:2). Prophets were seers, meaning they possessed supernatural insight or second sight or foresight. A seer was one who possessed divine insight and entered into the counsel of God and understood the plans of God, the ways of God, and the secrets of God.

Because the prophets were the custodians of the spiritual, civil social, economic, and political interests of God's people they were also known as "watchmen," "guardians," and even "patriots." They were God's "prosecuting attorneys" representing Divine interests in lawsuits against people, rulers, and nations. In Jeremiah 25:31, the prophet declared to the nation that, "The Lord hath a controversy with the nation, He will plead His case with all flesh." The language of Hosea 4:1 is very descriptive when the prophet declared; *"Hear the word of the Lord, ye children of Israel, for the Lord brings a charge against the inhabitants of the land."*

The call of individuals to function in the capacity of prophets was a Divine act initiated before birth or at any time during life. Jeremiah makes reference to being called before his birth (1:5). Samuel was dedicated to the service of the Lord by his mother before his birth and was reared in the house of Eli the priest (I Samuel 1-3). Amos referred to his call as though he was at least a young man: *"I was no prophet, neither was I prophet's son; but I was a herdsman, and a gatherer of sycamore fruit; and the Lord took me as I followed the flock and the Lord said unto me, 'Go, prophesy unto my people Israel'"* (Amos 7:14-15).

A noted emphasis of the prophet was intercessory prayer. The indispensability of prophetic intercession in the productive life and growth of Israel can be seen throughout the writings. The vested authority of the prayers of the prophets averted judgments, brought deliverance, and demonstrated a display of God's power. Such authority with God is so vividly demonstrated in a dialogue with Jeremiah when the Lord admonishes the prophet not to pray and cites references to past intercessions: *"Then said the Lord unto me, Though Moses and Samuel stood before Me, yet my mind could not be toward this people."* (Jeremiah 15:1) The Amplified version carries the impact of this verse little more vividly: *"Then the Lord said unto me, Though Moses and Samuel stood [interceding for them] before Me, yet My mind could not be turned with favor toward this people [Judah]."* In another dialogue, it seems apparent that the intercession of the prophet would surely avert judgment of the people so the Lord admonishes him not to pray:

1. Therefore pray not thou for this people, neither lift up a cry for them; for I will not hear them in the time that they cry unto me for their trouble. (Jeremiah 11:14, KJV)

2. Nor do thou, Jeremiah, think to intercede for this people of mine, or take up in their name the burden of praise and prayer. (Jeremiah 11:14, Knox)

3. You, for your part, must not intercede for this people of mine, nor raise either plea or prayer on their behalf. (Jeremiah 11:14, Jerusalem Bible)

The authority vested in the prophet to plead the cause of the people and to avert Divine judgment of their transgressions was a most significant function of the prophet.

The prophets were not infallible, and they possessed personal opinions. This is evidenced in a dialogue between Nathan the prophet and David concerning the possible building of a house for the Lord. David desires to build God a house and Nathan initially gives his own approval. But later the prophet is admonished by a Divine directive that counteracts this premature approval (II Samuel 7:1-17). Jeremiah records the fallibility of prophets:

> For both prophet and priest are profane; yea in my house have I found their wickedness, saith the Lord. Wherefore their way shall be unto them as slippery way in the darkness; they shall be driven on, and fall therein, for I will bring evil upon them, even the year of their visitation, saith the Lord. And I have seen the folly in the prophets of Samaria; they prophesied in Baal, and caused my people Israel to err. I have seen also the prophets of Jerusalem an horrible thing; they commit adultery and walk in lies; they strengthen also the hand of evildoers, that doth not return from his wickedness; they are all of them unto me as Sodom, and the inhabitants thereof as Gomorrah. Thus saith the Lord of hosts, Hearken not unto the words of the prophets that prophesy unto you; they make you vain; they speak a vision of their heart, and not out of the mouth of the Lord...I have not sent these prophets, yet they ran; I have not spoken to them, yet they prophesied.
>
> (Jeremiah 23:11-14, 16, 21)

The error of false prophets and the fallibility of true prophets is demonstrated (Chapter 3). All the terms used to describe the prophet indicate a close relationship of the prophet to God. Whether the prophet was interceding for the people, prophesying, or administering a Divine directive, the critical idea in all the definitions and explanations portray the prophet as a channel of Divine communication.

Prophecy, the message of the prophet, is not learned speech. It is an expression of Divine foreknowledge, intentions, purposes, and plans. Rebuke, reproof, counsel, and admonition can accompany its predictive element, therefore being corrective and instructive. Nathan the prophet corrects David after his seduction of Bathsheba when he declares, "Thou art the man!" (II Samuel 12:7). John the Baptist gives counsel and instruction for salvation when he declares, "Repent ye: for the kingdom of heaven is at hand" (Matthew 3:2). Prophecy is one of several channels of communicating divine information (I Corinthians 12:10, 39). The Apostle Paul lists prophecy among revelation, knowledge, and doctrine as an avenue of instruction (I Corinthians 14:6, 26). Prophecy expresses the will and the foreknowledge of God for an individual, group, or even a nation. It is important to acknowledge, however, that the foreknowledge of God and the will of God may not always be the same. Just because there is a Divine prediction of a future event does not grant that same event Divine approval. The Lord spoke unto Moses concerning Israel:

> *Now therefore write ye this song for you, and teach it to the children of Israel; put it in their mouths, that this song may be a witness for me against the children of Israel. For when I shall have brought them into the land which I sware unto their father, that floweth with milk and honey; and they shall have eaten and filled themselves, and waxen fat; then will they turn unto other gods, and serve them, and provoke me, and break my covenant.*

> *For I know thy rebellion, and thy stiff neck; behold, while I am yet alive with you this day, ye have been rebellious against the Lord: and how much more after my death? Gather unto me all the elders of your tribes and your officers, that I may speak these words in the ears, and call heaven and earth to record against them. For I know that*

> *after my death ye will utterly corrupt yourselves, and*
> *turn aside from the way which I have commanded you;*
> *and evil will befall you in the latter days; because ye will*
> *do evil in the sight of the Lord, to provoke him to anger*
> *through the work of your hands. (Deuteronomy 31:19-20,*
> *25-29)*

This was an expression of Divine foreknowledge of Israel's future transgression, but it was not an expression of the will of God for them to sin. Thus, the predictive element of prophecy is not always synonymous with the expression of Divine will, purposes, and intentions.

Paul includes prophecy as one of the channels of communicating and establishing the Church: "Now brethren, if I come unto you speaking with tongues, what shall I profit you, except I shall speak to you either by revelation, or by knowledge, or by prophecy or by doctrine?" (I Corinthians 14:6). From this statement it appears that prophecy is not a substitute for teaching sound doctrine or for imparting knowledge or revelation. Paul says that if he is to profit the Corinthians, he cannot simply prophesy to them, but he must teach and instruct them. Prophecy is not then an independent source of divine guidance nor a substitute for wisdom and knowledge that comes from sound Biblical preaching, teaching, counseling, and personal experience.

A distinction is often made between the gift of prophecy operating in the life of the believer and the prophetic ability of the prophet. A prophet will exhibit not only the gift of prophecy in a resident manner, but also other gifts such as word of knowledge, word of wisdom, discerning of spirits, and possibly even the power gifts of faith, miracles, and healing. All of the aforementioned gifts may not be operative in an individual prophet, but there are groupings. Paul addressed the issue of the prophet's ability of personal government in the management of prophetic ability by declaring that "the spirits of the prophets are subject to the prophets" (I Corinthians 14:32). The government of spiritual ministry in the individual believer is qualified with the phrase "as the spirit wills" (I Corinthians 12:11). This does not negate the responsibility of the individual believer to exercise discipline in discharging of ministry. But there is the proposition that the Holy Spirit may operate differently in the prophet and the individual believer. This is not a statement indicating a hierarchy of importance, but rather a proposition that there is a difference in the ministration.

Why does God use prophecy and when? Christ is the subject and objective of prophecy. Prophecy is the testimony of Jesus and His redemptive life and work, and His coming glory. The testimony of Jesus in the Book of Revelation is the declaration of the return of Christ to govern all things (Revelation 1:2). Hence, there is a sense in which prophecy is "eschatological" or an expression of "last day things." God uses predictive prophecy to give us a revelation of His eternal purposes and final judgments. However, the motive behind Divine activity is yet still a mystery. To presume to know why God intervenes in human affairs through the channel of prophecy is speculation. Yet, one-fourth of the Bible is filled with prophetic activity. God desires to communicate. Bishop Bill Hamon in his book on Prophets and Personal Prophecy, wrote that the prophets predicted and prepared the way for the coming of the Messiah and revealed the mysteries of eternal purposes for the Church.[3] Luke the apostle reminds us that "To Christ gave all the prophets witness" (Acts 10:43). The supreme revelation of Christ Jesus was announced by the prophets. Amos the prophet wrote that Divine announcements precede Divine activity (Amos 3:7). Although it is difficult to encapsulate all motivation for the channel of prophecy, it is obvious that Divine disclosure of eternal purposes and plans is a supreme motive. And even though prophecy may be instructive and corrective for an individual or even a people, there is still a greater function that prophecy plays in disclosing of eternal purposes and intentions.

PERSONAL PROPHECY

The eschatological dimension of prophecy is concerned with the unfulfilled predictions of "last day things." This aspect of prophecy is found in the New Testament and is related to the return of Christ for His Church and the establishment of eternal plans and final judgments. However, there is another dimension of prophecy that addresses the life of individual men today. This is called "personal prophecy" and is an expression of Divine foreknowledge, will, intentions, and plans for an individual, people, nation or world. Bishop Hamon defines personal prophecy as "specific information coming from the mind of God for a specific situation or an inspired word directed to a certain audience."[4]

Personal prophecy is conditional. That is, the fulfillment of personal prophecy is not totally dependent upon the faithfulness of God alone, but upon the faith and obedience of the recipient. The prophet Hosea declared: *"Then shall we know if we follow on to know the Lord"* (6:3). Revelation is never independent from obedience, which is always the door to spiritual revelation. The conditions of fulfillment are sometimes stated in the personal prophecy. Peter on the day of Pentecost declared: "Repent, and be baptized every one of you in the name of Jesus Christ for the remission of sins, and ye shall receive the gift of the Holy Ghost" (Acts 2:8). Fulfillment of this decree rested upon repentance, reordering of personal lifestyles, and living a life of faith and obedience to the revealed will of God.

In many instances, the individual's response to personal prophecy is predicated on knowing the ways, terminology, times, and seasons of God. For example, Divine terminology is quite interesting. Samuel said unto the rebellious Saul that *"the Lord hath rent the kingdom of Israel from thee this day, and hath given it to a neighbor of thine, that is better than thou"* (I Samuel 16:28). Note the phrase "this day" may have declared an immediate act in the economy of heaven, but it took years for the earthly events to take place. The Scriptures seem to indicate that a decree with the terms "now," "this day," or "immediately," does not exclude the existence of a process that may take a considerable period of time before the actual event takes place. Bishop Hamon makes an interesting observation concerning timetables based upon personal experiences:

- "Immediately" means from one day to three years.
- "Very soon" means one to ten years.
- "Now" or "this day" means 1 to 40 years.
- "I will" without a definite time designation means God will act sometimes in the person's life if he or she is obedient.
- "Soon" was the term Jesus used to describe the time of His soon return almost 2,000 years ago. He said, "Behold, I come quickly."[5]

Thus, timetables can be quite different from personal time frames.

Personal processes are likewise interesting. The ministry of Paul and the insight given to Ananias concerning the process of Paul's ministry development displays this point: Then Ananias answered, *"Lord, I have heard by many of this man, how much evil he hath done to thy saints at Jerusalem: And here he hath authority from the chief priests to bind all that call on thy name. But the Lord said unto him, Go thy way; for he is a chosen vessel unto me, to bear my name before the Gentiles, and kings, and the children of Israel: For I will show him how great things he must suffer for my name's sake."* Although the insight was clear concerning the ministry of Paul, there was a process of preparation and consequences of ministration yet to be revealed. Paul teaches us much about the process. In Romans 5:3, he writes that tribulation worketh patience; and patience, experience; and experience, hope. In the epistle to the Corinthians, he writes that a thorn in the flesh, a messenger of Satan, was given to buffet him to keep him humble (I Corinthians 12:7). In the epistle to the Philippians, he writes that he had learned to be content in whatsoever state he found himself. All this seems to indicate that certain personal decrees and promises were fulfilled through a process that took time.

The promises to individuals of faith, wisdom, and even prosperity are fulfilled through many experiences of difficulties, trials, and defeats. Once again, Paul is our teacher when he writes about the manifestation of the life of Jesus in her own body: We are troubled on every side, yet not distressed; we are perplexed, but not in despair; persecuted, but not forsaken; cast down, but not destroyed; always bearing about in the body the dying of the Lord Jesus, that the life also Jesus might be made manifest in our body (II Corinthians 4:8-10). Phases of negativity seem to precede phases of "positivity." Before faith, wisdom, love, and even ministry comes to be a reality, there are the periods of experience, which seem to be destructive but are the instruments of fulfillment.

Personal prophecy must be judged by eldership (I Corinthians 14:29). All spiritual utterances should be evaluated to determine their origin, content, and intent. This is absolutely necessary in order to determine a proper response to the prophetic utterance. Let us examine these parameters of judgment and establish the boundaries of appropriate responses.

Let us start with the source. Is the origin of the utterance from the Holy Ghost, demonic spirit, or human spirit? The Apostle John warned the Church not to believe every spirit, but to try them to determine if it is the Holy Ghost or an evil spirit (I John 4:1). But how is this done? Is it by the sound of the words? Is the judgment to be made by some internal "witness" that the hearer gets when the prophecy is coming forth? Well, there are several references that alert us to some form of delineating the true from the false:

1. *"Beware of false prophets which come in sheep's clothing, but inwardly they are ravenous wolves. Ye shall know them by their fruits. Do men gather grapes of thorns, or figs of thistles? Even so every good tree bringeth forth good fruit; but a corrupt tree bringeth forth evil fruit. A good tree cannot bring forth evil fruit, neither can a corrupt tree bring forth good fruit. (Matthew 7:16-18)"*

2. *"Hereby know ye the Spirit of God; every spirit that confesseth that Jesus Christ is come in the flesh is of God; and every spirit that confesseth not that Jesus Christ is come in the flesh is not of God; and this is that spirit of Antichrist whereof ye have heard that it should come, and even now already is it in the world. (I John 4:1-3)"*

3. *Whereof I give you to understand, that no man speaking by the Spirit of God calleth Jesus accursed; and that no man can say that Jesus is lord, but by the Holy Ghost. (I Corinthians 12:3)*

From these references it appears that the burden of judgment rests upon a group of factors. Jesus speaks of the fruit of the life and the ministry of the prophet. Fruits in the life of the prophet speaks of character, interpersonal relationships, and relationship with the corporate Body of Christ. Fruits of ministry speaks of the historical accuracy and the past productivity of the prophet or minister. Jesus does not separate the ministry of the prophet from the life of the prophet. The Apostle John validates or invalidates the source of the spiritual utterance by what is spoken. If the spirit acknowledges the humanity and the divinity of Jesus Christ, it is of God. Paul, likewise, places a singular emphasis upon the messenger's acknowledgment of the divinity of Jesus Christ. It appears that a composite picture is necessary.

If a prophetic minister comes into a town or city and declares he is sent by God, how is he to be evaluated? If he comes into the city unannounced and refuses to communicate or cooperate with the religious leaders in that city, how should he be evaluated? If he encourages people to come and support his meetings and yet refuses to meet with the elders of that city or town, what should be thought of him? If he has been accused of questionable character and exhibits a lifestyle that does not represent a standard to be emulated by other Christians, what should be the response to such a man? Be careful how you respond for there were similar allegations surrounding the life and ministry of Jesus. He kept company with publicans, harlots, and tax collectors. He was known not to submit to the elders of the towns, and he exhibited customs and ministry ethics that were highly disregarded by the religious leaders. Perhaps it would be advisable to move ahead further and examine other parameters to be used in judgment before settling on one area.

Let us examine the content of the message. Whatever is spoken should be comprehended. Paul instructed the prophets at Corinth to speak one at a time to avoid confusion (I Corinthians 14:29-33). Modem technology allows us to record personal utterances in order to evaluate the content later. It is true that the content of the utterance may or may not be of some doctrinal or theological significance. It may relate totally to the personal life of the individual and bare no reference to any doctrine or body of beliefs. If the utterance is in contradiction to orthodox truth or some established ethical or moral norm, then it can easily be discounted. If the prophecy denies the humanity and the divinity of Jesus or declares itself to be a higher revelation than the Scriptures, then it can easily be judged false. If the prophecy encourages ethical or moral behavior that is in obvious contradiction to established codes of Christian conduct, it can be dismissed immediately. However, much personal prophecy seems to deal with the life and at times, the ministry of the individual. It seems to outline promises, plans, and future developments involving ministry, geographic locations, travel, personal relationships, finances, buildings, and unexpected challenges to be experienced. How are these things to be judged?

Time and fulfillment is the validation of the authenticity of the content of prophecy (Jeremiah 23:13-40: John 13:19). But how is one to judge the content in the meanwhile? If there is a predictive element to an utterance, then time alone is the judge of its authenticity. If the content is confirmation of something already known, then that becomes the validation. And if the content is directive and instructs the hearer to respond in some manner, then there should be the involvement of counsel, personal discretion, and common sense. Directive content involving such areas of concern as marriage, employment, finances, possessions, geographic moves, relocation of ministry, changes in ministry relationships, or even travel should be kept in proper context with the revealed Word, sound counsel, experience, and practical wisdom and knowledge. Any content that contains directive elements regarding these or other related areas should be evaluated in the light of a consensus of other spiritual input, counsel, and personal discretion. But let us not dismiss content simply because it is new or contrary to personal opinions or conclusions. Prophecy is not simply conformational. This is not to presuppose that prophecy always transcends the witness of the individual's own personal understanding, but it is a setting forth of the proposition that there can be a revelational content in prophecy, especially when the prophet is speaking (Acts 11:27-28, 21:10-12). We will discuss this further as we determine the proper response to prophecy.

The intention of the prophetic utterance must be established. Is it edifying, exhorting, or comforting? Is it directive, corrective, or predictive? Does it liberate the hearer from faithlessness or despair, or does it enslave? Does it produce growth and maturity, or does it foster dependency and immaturity? Prophecy is not intended to be the singular source of guidance in the life of a believer. Nor is prophecy to be used to super-cede the personal desires, ambitions, and decisions of the individual. Prophecy is not a substitute for sound judgment. Once the contents of the prophecy is known, then the intention can be identified by determining the elements that are predictive, directive, corrective, or informative. This will be very helpful in determining the appropriate response.

The proper response to a prophetic utterance is another critical area of concern. Once a spiritual utterance has been validated as authentic, and its content and intent understood, there remains the need of the individual to respond. At this junction, it is necessary to clarify a few matters:

1. Personal prophecy does not replace Scriptures in giving guidance.

2. The sufficiency of Scriptures as the final, complete and infallible authority for faith, and practice is not replaced by personal prophecy.

3. Preaching, teaching, and prophesying words that are not an exact duplication of the Scriptures, while not violating the character of Scriptures, are not extra-biblical revelation.

4. Prophecy is not infallible and must be judged by eldership.

5. All Scripture is given by inspiration of God, and is profitable for doctrine, for reproof, for correction, and for instruction in righteousness.

6. The closed canon of Scripture is the measuring rod or the standard of the Christian faith and of all truth and practices.

7. The Scriptural admonition is to despise not prophesying, prove all things (not deny all things), and hold fast to that which is good.

8. The proposition of the Scriptures and the ministry of the Holy Spirit are not contradictory.

These statements I fully enumerate to ensure the proper place of personal prophecy in the life of the believer. Prophecy is not a substitute for the Scriptures, counsel, and personal discretion. But prophecy, like preaching, teaching, and all ministry of the Holy Spirit, must be kept in proper context with the Scriptures. In addition, several writers have made comments concerning spiritual utterances:

1. J. Rodman Williams:

"Prophecy can by no means be taken casually. Since it is verily God's message to His people, there must be serious and careful consideration given to each word spoken, and application made within the life of the fellowship. Also because of the ever present danger of prophecy being abused—the pretense of having a word of God—there is need for spiritual discernment."[6]

2. Dennis and Rita Bennett:

"We should also be careful of personal, directive prophecy, especially outside the ministry of a mature and submitted man of God. Unrestrained 'personal prophecy' did much to undermine the movement of the Holy Spirit which began at the turn of the century. Christians are certainly given words for one another 'in the Lord'... and such words can be most refreshing and helpful, but there must be a witness of the Spirit on the part of the person receiving the words, and extreme caution should be used in receiving any alleged directive or predictive prophecy. Never undertake any project simply because you were told to by presumed prophetic utterance or interpretation of tongues, or by a presumed word of wisdom, or knowledge. Never do something just because a friend comes to you and says: "The Lord told me to tell you to do thus and thus.' If the Lord has instructions for you, He will give you a witness in your own heart, in which case the words coming from a friend will be a confirmation to what God has already been showing you. Your guidance must also agree with scripture."[7]

3. Donald Gee:

"There are grave problems raised by the habit of giving and receiving personal messages of guidance through the gifts of the Spirit...Bible gives a place for such direction from the Holy Spirit...But it must be kept in proportion. An examination of the Scriptures will show us that as a matter of fact the early Christians did not continually receive such voices from heaven. In most cases they made their decisions by the use of what we often call 'sanctified common sense' and lived quite normal lives. Many of our errors where spiritual gifts are concerned arise when we want the extraordinary and exceptional to be made the frequent and habitual. Let all who develop excessive desire for 'messages' through the gifts take warning from the wreckage of past generations as well as of contemporaries…The Holy Scriptures are a lamp unto our feet and a light unto our path."[8]

4. John Nichol:

"To the Pentecostal, prophecy is entirely supernatural…The gift has strong support for its congregational use in the writings of St. Paul but what happened in the early days of the Pentecostal movement was that many preoccupied themselves with the acquisition and the demonstration of this gift, using it to correct, rebuke, foretell, and direct. Thus functioning as the voice of the Spirit, they placed greater emphasis upon themselves as prophets and upon their utterances than upon the leadership of the appointed pastor or in the instruction which the scriptures give."[9]

Personal prophecy must be kept in a proper context. Supernatural instruction cannot be the only vehicle of counsel, knowledge, and decisions. The Christian is not to live by bread alone (prophecy) but by every word that proceeds out of the mouth of God (preaching, teaching, counsel, personal experiences, rational thinking, and common sense). Major decisions should not be made without a proper assessment of all the parameters of sound judgment. The Scriptures declare that the testimony of two or more witnesses is sufficient for validation (Matthew 18:16; John 8:17). The use of a multitude of counsel is a wise practice in any matter. Consensus judgment and unanimous opinion is very valuable in formulating conclusions on any issue. A prophetic consensus is also invaluable. That is, if there are several valid utterances, which confirm a directive or predictive element in a prophecy, there is then some basis for a proper response of faith and obedience.

Concluding Remarks

Is God still using prophecy as a means of communication? This is an issue that continues to evoke controversy among some New Testament scholars. It is the topic of continuity and discontinuity. How much of the old continues into the new, and how much is replaced? The cessationists declare that prophecy and prophets were an Old Testament phenomena with continued manifestation in the first century Church only. The strength of their exegetical argument seems to rest upon a contextual statement made by Paul in the Corinthian epistle:

> *Charity never fails; but whether there be prophecies, they shall fail; whether there be tongues, they shall cease; whether there be knowledge, it shall vanish away, for we know in part, and we prophesy in pan. But when that which is perfect is come, then that which is in part shall be done away. (I Corinthians 13:8-10)*

The cessationists argue that the "perfect" refer either to the first coming of Christ or the time when the canon of Scriptures were complete. A simple paraphrase of Paul's words will correct this misconception: "Now," wrote Paul, "I know in part; but then (when the canon of the New Testament is completed) shall I know fully even as also I was fully known." The apostle was martyred before the New Testament was completed. Paul was speaking of himself when he said "then shall I know" and he looked forward to a time when his own limited knowledge would be complete. Clearly, he was anticipating the Second Coming of Christ Jesus when he wrote those words.

While the verse itself does not tell when these gifts will cease finally, the context does indicate it specifically, "When that which is perfect is come." The temporal clause here refers to an "indefinite future time."[10] "That which is perfect," according to G.G. Findlay, "comes with the Lord from heaven."[11] The Apostle Paul mentions nothing about the cessation in this life. The gifts are designed for the brief interval of this age of the imperfect and will cease to exist at the Second Coming of Christ.[12]

The Scriptures advocate a continuation of prophecy and the ministry of the prophet beyond the first century Church. In the epistle to the Corinthians, the Apostle gives some transcendent instructions for spiritual ministry including the operation of the prophets (14:29-32). In the Ephesian epistle, Paul vividly declares that the ministry of the prophet will be established in the Church with a definite termination marked by the word "until" (Ephesians 4:11-14). Paul saw the gifts and offices as a provision to equip believers for ministry until the Lord returned (I Corinthians 1:7).

The apostolic age began with the supernatural ministry of the Holy Ghost. And it is the clear testimony of the Scripture that the ministry of the Holy Ghost will continue throughout the life of the Church, ending only at the return of our Lord Jesus Christ.

Discussion:

1. Explain the ministry of a prophet.
2. Give three areas of evaluation of prophecy.
3. List at least seven examples of directive prophecies.
4. Explain the factors that should be involved when responding to directive personal prophecy.

5. Give several examples of inappropriate responses to personal prophecies.

6. Play a tape of a personal prophecy and evaluate the content, intent, and source.

7. Give several reasons when to discard a personal prophecy.

Notes

[1] Theophile Meek. *Hebrew Origins.* (New York: Harper; 1960) 147

[2] William F. Albright. *From the Stone Age to Christianity.* 2nd 3d. (New York: Doubleday Anchor Books, 1957) 231

[3] Bishop Bill Hamon, *Prophets and Personal Prophecy: Guidelines for Receiving, Understanding and Fulfilling God's Personal Word to You* (Shippensburg, PA: Destiny Image, 1987). p. 32

[4] Ibid, p. 32

[5] Ibid, p. 123

[6] J. Rodman Williams, *The Era of the Spirit* (Plainfield, N. J.: Logos, 1971), 21

[7] T. Dennis and Rita Bennett, *The Holy Spirit and You* (Kingsway, 1971), 107

[8] Donald Gee, *Spiritual Gifts in the Work of Ministry Today* (Gospel Publishing House, 1963), 51-52

[9] John Thomas Nichol, *Pentecostalism* (New York: Harper and Row, 1966), 77

[10] Howard M. Ervin, *Spirit Baptism: A Biblical Investigation* (Peabody, Mass: Hendrickson Publishers, 1987) 175

[11] G.G. Findlay, *St. Paul's First Epistle to the Corinthians*, ed. W. Robertson Nicoll, Vol. II The Expositor's Greek Testament (Grand Rapids: Eerdman, (n.d.). 900

[12] J. Moffatt, *The Moffatt New Testament Commentary* (New York: Harper and Brothers, (n.d.), 200

CHAPTER 6

Discerning Reformation, Refreshing and Religious Fads

This century has witnessed significant Charismatic activity and times of renewal. There was a re-emphasis upon the Holy Ghost Baptism, miracles, healing, and other tongues during the Pentecostal Movement of 1906. The Latter Rain Movement in 1946 and 1947 ushered in a restoration of laying on hands and prophecy for the identifying of one's place in the Body of Christ and for the impartation and activation of the gifts of the Holy Ghost. The Charismatic Movement exhibited a renewal and reunion of the universal Church as the Holy Ghost facilitated dialogue and fellowship across denominations of Catholics, Independents, Lutherans,

Methodists, Baptists, Mennonites, Episcopalians, Presbyterians, Pentecostals, Messianic Jews, and many others. During the 1970's there was strong emphasis on discipleship, family life, Church growth, faith, prosperity, and word teaching. During the 1980's the Holy Spirit demonstrated the reality that the Church was salt and light, and that Christians should be involved in politics, corporate management, entertainment, athletics, law, science, and every lawful profession as a witness and influence of the kingdom of God. Emphasis was placed upon the office of the prophet both as a local and translocal ministry. The 1990's have witnessed a renewal emphasis upon apostolic ministry, Church government, liturgical leadership development, and the mobilization of the saints for responsible ministry.

All of these movements exhibit principles and practices that are orthodox. However, there were some overstatements of principles and practices that went beyond the borders of orthodoxy. Historically, when neglected truths or practices are restored to a level of acceptance, there remains the possibility of an overstatement and a neglect of other foundational teachings. If the overemphasis is allowed to run its course, it can lead to heretical behavior and concepts, which will ultimately be rejected.

In this section we will examine some of the confusion and controversy surrounding Charismatic activity. We will endeavor to briefly discuss some principles that are necessary to distinguish between three categories: 1) spiritual reformation, 2) times of refreshing, and 3) faddish phenomena that is a creation of human ingenuity. These activities will be distinguished based upon their character, redemptive value, application, and duration.

SPIRITUAL REFORMATION

A spiritual reformation is a revival emphasis upon a neglected practice or principle that possesses Biblical significance. There may be times of corporate repentance, renewed religious zeal, large scale evangelism, protracted camp meetings, and even miraculous demonstration of Pentecostal activity accompanying times of reformation. But the central focus is the activity of Holy Spirit implementing Divine agendas of the Kingdom of God in the realm of the world. Such an expression of the providential activity of the Holy Spirit can have tremendous implications in every sphere of human existence. Generally speaking, reformational activity is universal in scope. Its origin may be localized, but its application and effect are not specific to a geographical area, population of people, or a particular period of time. The focus of a reformation can be reproduced by faith even after the spiritual and psychological dimensions have declined. Reformations are sustained by faith and diligence and not by emotional fervor. The principles or practices being revitalized can be validated by Biblical warrant. Even in the absence of explicit Scriptural references, there will be some principle, precept, or example in Scripture to authenticate the emphasis being reformed.[1] Reformational activity of the Holy Ghost precipitates unity, fellowship, and cooperation among the Churches. Although there may be some initial resistance and controversy, the ultimate benefits are eventually realized. Hence, reformation principles and practices are generally universal in their application, reproducible by faith, validated by some Biblical precept, principle or example, and capable of transcending the time frame of their renewal emphasis.

Reformations generally have positive and negative elements. The negative elements include the expressions of prohibition and abolition which tends to negate or censor customs, practices, beliefs or laws that are contrary to the laws of God. The positive elements include the periods of renewal and restoration when both historic forms and patterns may be blended with new truth. Thus reformation may represent a blend of the new and the old and times of destruction and times of construction.

There have been several restorational or reformational movements within the Church including the Protestant Reformation, Holiness Movement, Pentecostal Movement, Latter Rain Movement, and the Charismatic Renewnal.[2] Each of these restorational movements displayed spiritual manifestations and experiences that had been neglected or abandoned within the Church. For example, the central issue of the Reformation was the problem of authority displayed by the Papacy. The Papacy had long been established as the supreme authority in matters of doctrine and matters of discipline within the Church.[3] At the time of the Protestant Reformation, the primitive rites of the Church had almost been totally replaced with devotional piety filled with superstitions and the worship of saints and relics.[4] There was no congregational participation in worship.[5] There was no proclamation of the Word and the language used was not comprehensible to the people.[6]

The goal of the Reformers was the purification of worship from pagan practices, restoration of congregational participation, and the reformation of worship according to Biblical standards. The Protestant reformers agreed upon the doctrine of repentance from dead works, justification by faith, salvation by the grace of God, and the individual priesthood of the believer. These reformational principles and practices have proven to be universal in their application, permanent in duration, redemptive in character, and reproducible by the faith of the redeemed community. The principles and practices of the Protestant Reformation are among the foundational stones upon which a local

Church should be established. The Holiness Movement brought forth an emphasis upon sanctification, holiness of life in this present world, divine healing, and water baptism for believers only. [7] Such names as Wesley, Finney, Whitefield, Spurgeon, Sunday, Moody, and Edwards were some of the prominent spokesmen of that period. There were extremes of legalism and liberty ranging from the exclusion from worldly amusement, sports, and fashions to the license of grace to participation in all things.[8]

The Pentecostal Movement ushered in a re-emphasis upon the Holy Ghost and other tongues.[9] Names such as Charles Fox Parham and William J. Seymour were prominent in the beginning of this movement. The Azusa Street revival of Los Angeles in 1906-1909 under Seymour's leadership convinced untold thousands of Christians around the world that the long awaited "latter rain" outpouring had begun.[10] Believers were baptized in the Holy Ghost and the preaching of the Word was accompanied by miracles, healing, speaking with new tongues, and Gifts of the Holy Ghost.[11]

The Latter Rain Movement in 1948 followed the Pentecostal Movement. This movement contributed to the growth and maturity of the Church through a renewal emphasis upon laying on hands and prophecy for identifying one's place in the Body of Christ and for impartation and activation of the gifts of the Holy Ghost.[12] Teaching emphasized the five-fold ministry offices of the apostle, prophet, evangelist, pastor, and teacher. Prominent names during this period were William Branham, Oral Roberts, T.L. and Daisy Osborne, Gordon Lindsay, Kathryn Kuhlman, Kenneth Hagin, Jack Coe, William Freeman, and Harold Herman.[13]

The Charismatic Movement was an extension of the Latter Rain Movement. The term "Charismatic" was used to identify those ministers and individual Christians in the historic and evangelical denominational Churches who had received the gifts of the Holy Ghost.[14] The Holy Ghost was poured upon the historic Protestant and Catholic Churches. Many of the ministers in these Churches began speaking in tongues and moving in all of the restored truth and spiritual experiences. Theological dialogue was established between Roman Catholic Bishops and Southern Baptists, American Baptists, Lutherans, Methodists, Presbyterians, and Episcopalians.[15]

During the 1970's there was strong emphasis on discipleship, family life, Church growth, faith, prosperity, and word teaching.[16] There were extremes and controversies over the applications of the truths. Nevertheless, the Holy Ghost reemphasized the Biblical principles of overcoming faith, prosperity, faith healing, the power of the Word, and the necessity of a continual positive confession.[17]

The 1980's experienced the Holy Spirit's work to demonstrate the reality of the Church as an agent of redemption and the involvement of Christians in every lawful activity as a witness and influence of the Kingdom of God.[18] Christians were encouraged to enter into professions of law, government, corporate management, science, and entertainment. Emphasis was placed upon the Kingdom of God, dominion theology, and reconstructionism. Prominent during that period was the ministry and teaching of Bishop Earl Paulk of Chapel Hill Harvester Church in Decatur, Georgia.[19]

The Prophetic Movement was also launched during the 1980's. It was a time of emphasis upon the ministry of the prophet both as a local and translocal ministry. Notable in that work was the ministry of Bishop Bill Hamon of Christian International Ministries in Point Washington, Florida.[20] Teaching and training about prophetic ministry and personal prophecy were prevalent activities.

During the 1990's there was an emphasis upon apostolic ministry in the government and function of the Church. Historic and contemporary liturgical patterns in worship were introduced as important themes as the Church sought to blend traditional styles of worship, structure, and the liberty of the Pentecostal experience. This period of time witnessed an effort to blend traditions from the Charismatic, Evangelical, and the Liturgical/Sacrmental.[21]

Each of these movements experienced extremes in their practices and theologies. Conflicts and controversies have been prevalent as leaders and ministries have struggled over the reformative process. Yet, there were genuine efforts to create channels of communication and cooperation around world evangelism, missions and charismatic renewal, and around public concern such as famine, abortion, and ecological problems. Networking trends provided a powerful tool of unifying various ministries into a mutual effort.

TIMES OF JOY, LAUGHTER AND REFRESHING

During the social upheaval in South Africa, several pastors reported an unusual sensation occurring in their congregations. Spontaneous laughter and great joy was occurring among the people during their times of worship without any obvious reason or solicitation. The people would laugh with such intensity as to literally fall to the floor. Similar events were reported in Australia, Canada, and the United States. Spontaneous laughter would engulf whole congregations for weeks and months at a time. There were reports of healing, deliverances, and other miraculous events occurring during these outbreaks of laughter. Some leaders who visited these events began to praise God and judge it as a divine visitation of the Holy Ghost. Others condemned the events as mass hysteria engineered by human suggestions.

Events such as laughter, joy, shouting, slaying in the spirit were reported in many Old and New Testament references. Whenever people encountered God or witnessed the benefits of His blessings, they sometimes fell down before Him, rejoiced exceedingly, and shouted with great joy. In some instances the experience was followed by visions and revelations of things to come. Perhaps it would be fruitful to examine some of these Biblical parallels.

Slaying in the Spirit. The Church has been quite cautious about reports of healing, visions, prophecies, miracles, hearing voices, or sensing supernatural manifestations. This caution, is probably more related to the sensationalism and fanaticism that accompanied some reports rather than to a total disbelief in the possibility of direct contact with God. Old and New Testament references reveal people who interacted with God. Similar experiences were well documented in the days of the revivals of the eighteenth and nineteenth centuries.[22] The ministries of highly visible personalities such as Kathryn Kuhlman, William Branham, Kenneth Hagin, Oral Roberts, and Benny Hinn have exposed the twentieth century to the experience of the Holy Ghost.[23]

Let us take a look at one event, that of "slaying in the spirit." Slaying in the spirit is an unusual and powerful phenomenon that is not without biblical parallels. Among Pentecostal and charismatic circles, the concept is known by various names, such as "overcome by the spirit," "falling under the power," and "resting in the spirit." The Hebrew word most frequently used to describe the experience is "naphal" which means to cast down, cease, die, to fall, to lie down, and to be overwhelmed.[24] The Greek word "pipto" carries the similar meaning to fall or fall down.[25]

When people encountered God, they sometimes fell down before

His presence; and in some instances, the experience was followed by visions or revelations. The Scripture does not report if this sense of being in the presence of God is a result of the power of His presence or a cultural gesture of prostrating oneself in obeisance. The Bible does not record if this falling down before God was a conscious act of fear or adoration, or if the individual had been struck down by the sheer power of God's presence. It is clear that the Biblical text records that when people encountered God, they responded by falling to the ground. For example, Abraham fell upon his face when God appeared to him and revealed that Sarah would bring forth a son in her old age (Genesis 17:3,17). There are other accounts of saints of God falling upon their faces in the presence of a visitation of God such as Aaron (Leviticus 9:24), Joshua (Joshua 5:14), and Daniel (Daniel 8:15-26).

In the New Testament the experience is essentially the same when saints encountered the presence of God. People fell down before Jesus, such as the woman who touched his robe and was healed (Mark 5:33), the Syro-Phenician woman (Mark 7:25), the Gerasene demoniac (Luke 8:28), and the boy tormented by a spirit (Mark 9:20).

The soldiers who came to arrest Jesus in the garden of Gethsemane fell backward and dropped to the ground when they came to arrest him (John 18:6). Three of the disciples were overwhelmed on the Mount of Transfiguration after hearing a voice from heaven, and they fell to the ground on their faces in fear (Matthew 17:6). The guards at the tomb of Jesus were struck down as dead men in the presence of an angel (Matthew 28:4).

The Apostle Paul recounts his conversion on the road to Damascus as an experience of falling to the ground after hearing a voice and seeing a great light (Acts 9:3-6, 22:6-10, 26:12-16). John speaks of falling down as if he were dead at hearing the voice of the Son of God (Revelation 1:17). It seems evident from the biblical texts that people were impacted by the divine presence of God. Whether their response was in awe or fear, conscious adoration, or a cultural pattern, it did occur.

The contemporary crisis that is presented is one of discovering a perspective. It would be quite easy to slander experiences or concepts that are outside our sphere of orthodoxy. There has been a significant history of that type of narrow scholarship. I think that the admonition of the Apostle Paul to the Corinthian Church expresses the context of concern when he said, "Let everything be done decently and in order." I realize that some quote this passage to censor freedom in spiritual activity. You cannot get involved with the Holy Ghost without discovering that you are an emotional creature and that you desire to worship God with the fullness of your psycho-physical capabilities. The scandal of our crisis is that we allow extreme religious practices to continue outside the realm of Church leadership or government. There is spiritual protocol, and we must not only be aware of it, but also enforce it.

Practices that are an expression of Biblical normality can become spiritual antagonists without proper discernment of the place and time for their expressions. Paul corrected the Corinthians in their expression of irresponsible spiritual freedom:

> *Brethren be not children in understanding; howbeit in malice be ye children, but in understanding be men. In the law it is written, With men of other tongues and other lips will I speak unto this people; and yet for all that they will not hear me, saith the Lord. Wherefore tongues are for a sign, not to them that believe, but to them that believe not; but prophesying serveth not for them that believe not, but for them which believe. If therefore the whole church be come together into one place, and all speak with tongues, and there are those that are unlearned, or unbelievers, will they not say that ye are mad? But if all prophesy, and*

*there come in one that believeth not, or one unlearned, he
is convinced of all, he is judged of all; and thus are the
secrets of his heart made manifest; and so heart made
manifest; and so falling down on his face he will worship
God, and report God is in you of a truth. How is it then,
brethren? When ye come together, every one of you hath
a psalm, hath a doctrine, hath a tongue, hath a revelation,
hath an interpretation. Let all things be done unto edifying. (I Corinthians 14:20-26)*

Several issues are represented here. One is the evangelistic dimension in our worship. We literally teach people about God and perhaps
introduce them to Him in the presentation of our worship. Paul declares that if an unbeliever or an unlearned person comes among a
gathering of saints worshiping God in the liberty of their expressions
without any structural restraint, it is confusing. He does not repri-
mand their zeal, but he does call into question their structural irre-
sponsibility. The Apostle's desire is to call them to a corporate concern
for every worshiper and even the believer. He presents the principle of
"edifying" which means to build up, instruct, and fortify. The individual liberty of the believer should not be expressed at the expense of the
whole Church. Whatever is done publicly should enhance the spiritual
climate of the whole assembly.

In our Pentecostal and Charismatic worship services, people are
encouraged to participate and be expressive. People are encouraged to
shout, dance, sing, laugh, and fall under the power, and to let go of
every psycho-physical restraint. Unfortunately, those who do not enter
into this experience are often judged and considered to be in bondage.

Whatever expression or experience that is encouraged in worship
should be evaluated on the basis of its fruit and put in a proper perspective with the intent of the worship experience.

There are some significant questions to be addressed such as:

1. Does the experience promote spiritual, emotional, and intellectual growth?

2. Are there any healing benefits to the individual's body, mind, and soul?

3. Does the experience build the faith, hope, and confidence of the participant?

4. Does the experience develop an unhealthy addiction or dependency in the individual?

5. Is the experience a form without true Pentecostal power?

The answer to such questions may prove to be helpful in assessing the spiritual and Biblical integrity of such experiences. Leaders who encourage certain expressions or experiences among the congregations of the saints should also be responsible to instruct them in governmental issues in order to avoid excesses and abuses. Leaders should also examine their own motives in encouraging the saints and be on guard against any practice or experience that would retard the growth and development of God's people.

Joy and Laughter. The Apostle Paul defined the Kingdom of God as "righteousness, joy, and peace in the Holy Ghost." This ingredient of "joy" as an incarnational benefit was promised to the disciples of Jesus during his discourse about the coming of the Holy Ghost:

> Verily, verity I say unto you, that ye shall weep and lament, but the world shall rejoice; and ye shall be sorrowful, but your sorrow shall be turned into joy. A woman when she is in travail hath sorrow, because her hour is come; but as soon as she is delivered of the child, when

remembereth no more the anguish, for joy that a man is born into world. And ye now therefore have sorrow; but I will see you again, and your heart shall rejoice, and your joy no man taketh from you. And in that day ye shall ask me nothing. Verily, verily, I say unto you, whatsoever ye shall ask the Father in my name, he will give it you. Hitherto have ye asked nothing in my name; ask, and ye shall receive, that your joy may be full. (John 16:20-24)

After Phillip went down to the city of Samaria and preached "things concerning the kingdom of God, and the name of Jesus Christ," and men and women were baptized, it is recorded that there was great joy in that city (Acts 8:8). When Paul came down to Antioch in Pisidia, it is recorded that the Jews mocked while the Gentiles were glad, and the disciples were filled with joy, and with the Holy Ghost (Acts 13:14-52,15:3). There was unbridled happiness among the disciples when they heard the gospel preached and received the Holy Ghost. The Greek word for "joy" in all these instances is "chara" which means "cheerfulness, exceeding joyfulness and gladness."[26] There can be no spiritualizing of this fact; this joy was the opposite of glum, despair, and oppression. These were happy and joyous people. And the Scriptures prescribe laughter and joy as beneficial medicine long before the health profession (Proverbs 17:22).

There is a more grave explanation to be given to laughter that has its origin in the Holy Ghost. Laughter is an expression of divine indignation over the senseless raging and threatening of heathens (Psalms 2:4, 37:13, 59:8). It is an expression of utter disdain of a higher authority to futile expressions of a lesser entity. When heathens threaten to destroy the works of God and seek to govern their lives apart from God, "He that sitteth in the heaven shall laugh" (Psalms 2:4). Divine laughter precedes divine judgment. Once the rebellion has reached its fullest expression, He who sits in the heaven does not begin to wring his hands and rub his brow in nervous anticipation. Before divine response is expressed fully, there is the contemptible scorn of laughter. It is a laughter of amusement and even entertainment over the futile efforts of a created entity attempting to engage the possibility of a successful campaign against the Creator.

Now if divine laughter precedes judgment, how do we assess the matter of Psalm 2? The heathen is organizing devices and schemes in an effort to silence the representative voice of God. Organizations and coalitions of unrighteousness are seemingly thriving. The airways are filled with the propaganda of a successful campaign because there has been no obvious response from heaven. But then there is a sudden expression of divine displeasure. The Psalmist describes it this way: "Then shall he speak unto them in his wrath, and vex them in his sore displeasure" (2:5). The response to this earthly silliness is both verbal and militant.

I took the time to develop this concept of joy and laughter as both an incarnational benefit to the people of God and as a divine expression of displeasure toward unrighteousness. The reason for this treatment was initially a personal search to bring meaning concerning the numerous reports of spontaneous laughter and joy among the Churches. In many of those meetings there were reports of healing, deliverances from evil spirits, restoration of broken relationships, and even salvations. These by-products are not strange to revivalism. However, running parallel to these positive evaluations have been reports that these manifestations of emotionalism and mass hysteria were products of hypnosis and thought suggestions by crafty leaders. So let us take a brisk stroll through history.

Great revivals have generally sprung up in times of moral and spiritual decline.[27] A review of Biblical history reveals that there were times of gross darkness that preceded the revivals under Asa (II Chronicles 15:1-15), Hezekiah (II Chronicles 29-31), Josiah (H Kings 22,23), Zerubbabel (Ezra 5,6), and Nehemiah (Nehemiah 8:9, 12:44-47). In the presence of idolatry, apostasy, and entanglement of the leaders and the people with heathen nations, there were those who earnestly sought the Lord for revival (II Chronicles 7:13-14).

Post-Civil War America was seething in hostility and economic decline. Population migration to the cities and lack of immediacy.[28] Corrupt bureaucracy and the unequal distribution of wealth and opportunity established distinct communities of rich and poor.[29] The Churches were populated with exponents of liberal theology and higher criticism of the Bible.[30] The deity of Christ, the virgin birth, and the substitutionary atonement were being rediculed.[31] Another gospel was transcending the witness of the apostolic preaching.[32]

In the presence of such deteriorating world conditions, there was an outpouring of the Holy Ghost and evident revival. The by-products of such revival was joy, miraculous healing, deliverances, and transformed lives. Charles H. Conn, in his book Like a Mighty Army, a history of the Church of God, described one of the early revivals:

> *"Enthusiasm remained high. The services were generally of an emotional nature-yet the stabilizing influence of teaching, while far from adequate, was not altogether absent. The emotion that made the worshipers weep, laugh, and shout was not some indefinable psychological delirium; it stemmed from the exaltation they received from a sense of the presence of God."* [33]

The Presbyterians came under the influence of the Second Great Awakening, which began in the Cane Ridge, Kentucky area in 1801. William Sweet, in his book, Revivalism in America, records that at the Cane Ridge camp meeting thousands of people would fall in the state of a trance, and hundreds were given to such demonstrations as "jerking, rolling, dancing, and barking."[34]

A casual visitor to the Azusa Street revival would have been awestruck. Men and women would shout, dance, speak in tongues, fall into trances, and give interpretation to tongues in English.[35] The frenzy of religious zeal was contagious.[36]

Laughter, shouting, speaking in tongues, interpreting tongues, trances, barking, jerking, and rolling are just a small list of other reported human responses to Holy Ghost activity. [37] Tongues and interpretation of tongues are listed among the diversities of gifts of the Spirit (I Corinthians 12:7-10). The others are referred to as consequences of "times of refreshing."

The issue is one of perspective and not censorship. The psycho-physical dimension of the worship experience must be placed in context with the other ingredients of worship such as the ministry of the Word, Eucharist, and Baptism. The freedom of the individual believer must be placed in relationship to the edification of the corporate body of believers. And some determination of what is normal or sensational should be made. The ministry of the Holy Ghost as teacher, guide, and enabler, and the mission of the Church in the world should be kept as a constant reminder to every member of the Body of Christ. If this does not occur, then congregational meetings will degenerate into entertainment sessions.

RELIGIOUS FADS

Fads are practices or interests which are followed or emulated for a period of time with exaggerated zeal and popularity and then abandoned. They are prevailing customs, usage, or styles, which influence the behavior and lifestyles of a population. Fads are contemporary standards of behavior, dress, or conduct that represent a break with some historic norms or a recurrence of some old patterns once discarded. These patterns of contemporary practices or interests may exhibit their influence in every aspect of human involvement ranging from politics, religion, sports, education, family life, entertainment, and fashions. The degree of importance attached to a fad depends upon the extent of public interest and emulation of the practice or principle. This is readily seen in the clothing industry when a contemporary fashion design takes on a broad audience appeal. In the area of entertainment, there are cycles of interests in jazz, classical, rhythm and blues, and country music that are reflected in the popularity charts. These pulsating and migrating streams of interest that have their times of appearance, popularity, and decline are referenced as fads.

The character of a fad may range from harmful to harmless. During the 1960's the emergence of youthful revolts against authority and against any established norm took on a faddish dimension. Many young people, especially among the colleges and universities, demonstrated their political and social views through protests and a social truancy in which they detached themselves from many mainline traditions. Fashions, music, and hair became a noticeable badge of commitments to the "new generation." The mark of identity with "the struggle" was, among other things, conformity with the established "pop culture."[38]

Although fads are generally a social phenomenon, they can touch every facet of human behavior. My particular interest is in Christian experience. I am quick to admit that in our efforts to be contemporary salt and light and relevant witnesses in the world, there is a need for changes in the methods and practices of evangelism, music, and social programs. The Holy Spirit inspires us with innovative methods and strategies to extend the influence of the Kingdom of God. As Christians, we do pursue practices and interests with an exaggerated zeal for periods of time and then abandon them. These areas of zealous interests may range from music, forms of worship, to methods of evangelism. These cycles of interests and practices exhibit various degrees of popularity and longevity. The critical interest is the origin of the interest or practice. There are cycles in which the Holy Spirit operates in certain areas. But there are also practices and principles that are products of human ingenuity and creativity. This does not make these principles or practices demonic. But it raises a question of perspective. What is the comparative value and interest that should be given to such principles or practices? How can we offer some guidelines to maintain proper religious focus and prevent these cycles of interests and practices from becoming a substitute for Biblical foundations? Hence, there is some importance in distinguishing between a religious fad, a spiritual reformation, and a time of refreshing.

There are certain characteristics of religious fads, which may or may not be consistent:

1. They are geographically or situationally specific. They may occur or operate in a certain geographic area or among a specific group of people but lack universal application. They normally cannot be validated by Biblical evidence. The attention given to the concept or practice is not in keeping with such manifestations or practices seen in the Scriptures.

2. They cannot be reproduced by faith. Since they are the products of human ingenuity, imagination, and will, they cannot be equally duplicated by other believers.

3. They generally promote disunity or competition. Although they initially appear to serve as a rallying point of activity, they ultimately foster behavioral and operational conflicts.

4. They have no significant "after effect." Once the human zeal and interest has dissipated, there is no lasting benefit.

5. The duration of fads is time-dated. The attention and popularity given to the fad is measured in months and not years.

Every spiritual reformation has been accompanied by its share of eccentric and ecstatic behavior. True revivalism has often sparked Biblical practices that became popular long after the fervor of the season had passed. Various beliefs and practices of the Latter Rain found their way into the Charismatic Renewal, including spiritual singing and dancing, praise, the foundational ministries of Ephesians 4:11, the laying on of hands, tabernacle teaching, and the foundational truths of Hebrews 6:1-2.[39]

The critical concern is the negative effect such practices can exert upon the reformative process. Acceptable principles and practices that are extended beyond the range of their purpose can become sensational and even fanatical. All things may be lawful, but all things may not be expedient. Even individual freedom of expression that is exercised at the expense of the corporate freedom of a group can become lawless. If faddish behavior is closely aligned with the genuine activity of the Holy Ghost, it may warrant some definitive acts of separation. If on the day of Pentecost the crowd that gathered around the disciples who had recently received the Holy Ghost had heard them speak with tongues, prophesy, and saw them walking on their hands and knees, what would they have concluded? They would have concluded that this Spirit baptism must also necessitate walking on your hands and knees. And so when Paul would come to the coast of Ephesus, he would have asked the disciples of John, "Have you received the Holy Ghost with the evidence of walking on your hands and knees?" This is taking a lot of liberty with the Scriptures, but it represents the crisis we face constantly. Activities and practices that have no Biblical validation and meet the criteria of a fad should not be considered foundational to the Christian faith nor to any ministry. My plea is for spiritual judgment, so that as Christians, we do not close the door on the very world we are at tempting to reach because of nonsensical behavior. If the Holy Ghost is not behind the practice or concept, then let us acknowledge that it is either a product of human ingenuity or demonic. However, let us not say anything at all. Lack of involvement in the judging of spiritual matters is not an option.

The critical issues can be summarized in a few statements:

1. Principles and practices that have no redemptive value and cannot be reproduced by faith may be observed by a local assembly, but should not be considered as a foundation of ministry.

2. Principles and practices that cannot be validated universally in their application should be regarded carefully and given their proper significance or insignificance in a ministry.

3. Biblically valid principles and practices alone should serve as foundation of ministry.

4. Principles and practices should not simply be rejected nor declared false simply because they are outside of our sphere of orthodoxy.

5. Eccentric behavior and questionable practices should not be the only basis of invalidating a particular movement.

6. Principles and practices that are redemptive in value, reproducible by faith, universal in their application, and validated by some Biblical precept or example should be considered reformative in character.

7. Principles and practices that are geographically and situationally specific, non- exportable, Biblically validated, sovereignly initiated and terminated, should be considered as times of refreshing.

8. Principles and practices that are not redemptive in character, localized in their application, and not reproducible by the universal faith community should be carefully examined for their contribution to the growth, unity, health, and mission of the Church.

There is a great need for patience, tolerance, and discernment in these matters. To scandalize activities that exist outside of our denomination or sphere of influence is a contradiction of the Christian faith. We should be aware and responsive to the work of the Holy Spirit in bringing different religious "streams" and denominations together. Let us utilize all the truth and remain committed to basic doctrinal principles and practices, which have been summarized, in the great creedal statements of the Church, such as the Apostles' Creed and the Nicene Creed. Let us maintain a proper balance between experiential theology (visions, dreams, revelations, prophecies, etc.) and propositional theology (Scriptures and the creedal statements). Jesus stated the issue more succinctly in a parable of two foundations:

Whosoever cometh to me, and heareth my sayings, and
foundation on a rock; and when the flood arose, the stream

*beat vehemently upon the house, and could not shake it;
for it was founded upon a rock. But he that heareth; and
doeth not, is like a man that without a foundation built an
house upon the earth; against which the stream did beat
vehemently, and immediately it fell; and the ruin of that
house was great. (Luke 6:47-49)*

Notes

[1] James B. Jordan, *The Sociology of the Church* (Geneva Ministries: Tyler, TX copyright 1986)

[2] Bill Hamon, *The Eternal Church* (Phoenix, Arizona: Christian International, 1981) pp.158

[3] John Henry Collins, *Basis and Belief* (London: The Epworth Press, 1964) pp.57-62

[4] Kenneth Latourette, *A History of Christianity* (New York: Harper and Rowe, 1975) pp.995-998

[5] Ibid.

[6] Ibid

[7] Bill Hamon, *The Eternal Church* (Phoenix, Arizona: Christian International, 1981) pp. 187-208

[8] Ibid

[9] Ibid

[10] Ibid

[11] Ibid

[12] Richard M. Riss, *The Latter Rain* (Ontario, Canada: Kingdom Flagship Foundation, 1987) pp. 11-12

[13] Stanley M. Burgess and Gary B. McGee, *Dictionary of Pentecostal and Charismatic Movements* (Grand Rapids: Zondervan Publishing House, 1988) pp. 222, 345, 361, 529, 540

[14] Ibid 1

[15] Ibid

[16] Kirby Clements, *A Philosophy of Ministry* (Decatur, Georgia: Harvester Booksellers, 1993) p. 12

[17] Ibid

[18] Ibid

[19]Earl Paulk, *The Provoker* (Decatur, Georgia: Harvester Booksellers, 1992) p.12

[20]Bill Hamon, *Prophets and the Prophetic Movement* (Shippensburg, PA: Destiny Image, 1990) pp.59

[21]Kirby Clements, *A Philosophy of Ministry* (Decatur, Georgia: Harvester Booksellers, 1993) pp. 13-14

[22]Stanley Fordsham, *With Signs Following* (Springfield, Missouri: Gospel Publishing House, 1946) pp.19

[23]Stanley M. Burgess and Gary B. McGee, *A Dictionary of Pentecostal and Charismatic Movements* (Grand Rapids: Zondervan Publishing House, 1988) p. 420

[24]Geoffrey M. Bromley, *Theological Dictionary of the New Testament* (Grand Rapids: Eerdmans, 1985)

[25]Ibid

[26]Ibid

[27]Kenneth S. Latourette, *A History of Christianity* (New York Harper & Row; 1975 pp. 349-1408)

[28]Ibid

[29]Ibid

[30]Ibid

[31]Ibid

[32]Ibid

[33]Charles H. Conn, *Like A Mighty Army* (Cleveland, Tennessee: Pathway Press, 1977)

[34]William Sweet, *Revivalism in America* (Cleveland, Tennessee: Pathway Press, 1967)

[35]Ibid

[36]Ibid

[37]Ibid

[38]My personal reflections as a contemporary of the 1960's and a witness of the social movement.

[39]Richard M. Riss, *The Latter Rain* (Ontario, Canada: Flagship Foundation, 1987) p. 141

CHAPTER 7

Discernment and Body Life

I n this section we will examine corporate worship patterns of the Christian communities. Our objective is to determine the influence of worship patterns upon the growth of the local Church. We will use the tool of discernment to explore the influence of culture, religious backgrounds of members, and the various concepts of worship that exist.

Corporate worship of God is regularly performed by all the various expressions of Christianity. Although the object of worship may be consistent among the various branches of the Christian community, the mode and manner of worship varies. In some Church communities, worship is circumscribed by hymnals, creeds, and printed orders of worship; while in other circles, there are no written orders to follow. The atmosphere of the worship experience ranges from unbridled enthusiasm to quiet, solemn reverence. The music of celebration and adoration ranges from hymns, psalms, revelational songs, and cantatas to rock and even jazz.

There are cultural influences that appear in the worship experiences. The Scriptures encourage the lifting of hands, dancing, shouting, and vocal participation during times of corporate worship, but the manner in which this is done may vary among different cultures and ethnic groups, suggesting that some of the human expressions in worship are learned or acquired. The manner of human expressions and the various degrees of emotionalism may reflect a behavior that is not genetic or peculiar to a particular race, but a behavior that is acquired from the religious environment. The various human responses during times of corporate worship are based upon what the individual or the group believes the Scriptures demand.

A critical fact to remember is that the experience of worship did not begin in this century, nor is it a peculiar function of a specific denomination. Worship is a re-enactment of a historic drama of God interacting with His people. Consequently, there is a Biblical basis for the character and nature of the worship experience. In the celebration of the Eucharist, water baptism, offering of prayers, preaching, teaching, giving tithes and offerings, and the singing of psalms, hymns, and spiritual songs, there is a re-statement of historic truths recorded in our rich Judeo-Christian heritage. With this fact in mind, it may be profitable to briefly explore some of our heritage to discover parallels and differences between contemporary and historical faith communities.

HISTORICAL WORSHIP

The Apostle John records a very interesting conversation that occurred between Jesus and an unknown Samaritan woman. The dialogue began over the issue of water and evolved into a revelation of worship that directs us today:

The woman saith unto him, *"Sir, I perceive that thou are a prophet. Our fathers worshiped in this mountain; and ye say, that in Jerusalem is the place where men ought to worship."* Jesus saith unto her, *"Woman, believe me, the hour cometh, when ye shall neither in this mountain, nor yet at Jerusalem worship the Father. Ye worship ye know not what; we know what we worship; for salvation is of the Jews. But the hour cometh, and now is, when the true worshipers shall worship the Father in spirit and in truth. God is a spirit; and they that worship him must worship him in spirit and in truth"* (John. 4:19-24).

This conversation dismissed the idea that worship had to be in a specific place. Although Jesus did not give an order of worship, He was very empathic about the requirements for the experience. The present form of worship would undergo a radical change, and "the hour cometh" when the acceptable worship of God would be established.

Jesus expressed that Old Testament forms of worship ultimately focused on Him. Even though He respected the temple and its place in the worship experience of the Jews, He expressed the beginning of a transition when He referred to Himself as "one greater than the temple" (Matthew 12:6). He applied Old Testament Scriptures to Himself with statements such as "this day this scripture is fulfilled in your ears" (Luke 4:21). And when He openly broke the rules of the Sabbath (Mark 2:27-28) and challenged the regulations regarding fasting and prayer (Matthew 6:5-8,16-18), Jesus was exercising His right to redefine Jewish worship.

Since Christianity began among the Jews and spread eventually to the Gentiles, it is interesting to note that each of these groups injected cultural influences into the evolving New Testament worship. The

Jewish Christians were caught in a transition between Old Testament worship patterns and Christianity. This is evidenced by Paul's letter to the Galatians in which he argued that the law was a "schoolmaster to bring us into Christ" (3:24-25) and that the converts should not return to the "weak and beggarly elements" (4:9) nor avail themselves to circumcision (5:6). Of course, the differentiation between Christianity and Jewish worship was clearly set forth in Hebrews. The new interpretation of the temple, priesthood, sacrifices, and the Passover lamb, along with the identification of these elements with the Church, was indeed radical and clearly established the break between Christianity and Jewish worship.

The Gentiles lacked the rich heritage of the Jews. The early evidence of the cultural influences in their worship is seen in the epistle to the Corinthians. It appeared that the Gentile converts needed to be instructed in the manner of public worship. Their desire for freedom was evidenced in their ecstatic expressions (I Corinthians 14:26-40). When Paul wrote to the Corinthian church, he emphasized more of the content of worship rather than the sequence. Although he clearly stated that everything ought to be done "decently and in order," he seemed to focus on the various aspects of the worship experience as being: (a) psalms, doctrine, tongues, revelation, and interpretation of tongues (I Corinthians 14:26); (b) revelation, knowledge, prophesy, and doctrine (I Corinthians 14:6); and (c) prayer, singing, giving thanks, and expressions of Amen (I Corinthians 14:13-19).

The ingredients of early Christian worship included not only reading, proclamation, confession, prayer, doxology, blessing, singing hymns and psalms, prophecies, speaking with tongues and interpretation of tongues, and special gifts of the Holy Ghost, but also the breaking of bread (Acts 2:42,46; 20:7). There was a balance between

Word (preaching, teaching, prayer, proclamation, prophecies, singing psalms and hymns, and speaking with tongues) and breaking of bread; each was maintained as a dual emphasis. The pattern of Jewish Synagogue worship was exclusively a service of the Word (reading Scriptures, preaching, prayer, blessing, singing of psalms). A significant break between Jewish and Christian worship was represented by, though not limited to, the Eucharistic meals. Here again the Christian proclamation that Messiah had come and a re-enactment of such a belief was indeed a decisive factor in this break.

The significance of the Eucharistic meal was viewed in its association with the celebration of the resurrection, the thought of the Last Supper, the presence of Christ in the midst of the community gathered for the meal, and the anticipation of His coming again. The idea of Christ's death was balanced with the knowledge of His resurrection. I dare think today that the death of Christ is so emphasized that the valuable connection between the resurrection, the Lord's Supper, and the anticipated coming of the Lord is almost lost (I Corinthians 11:26).

A critical fact in the pattern of early Christian worship was the maintenance of the balance between Word and Spirit. The exercise of spiritual gifts was allowed as long as the Church was edified. The edification of the worshiping community seemed to have been an essential purpose of the gathering (I Corinthians 14). Paul insisted that freedom and order were both compatible attitudes of the Holy Ghost (I Corinthians 14:40). And though Paul insisted that the community should critically examine the use of spiritual gifts (I Corinthians 14:29; I Thessalonians 5:19), he encouraged them not to "quench the Spirit." The liturgical emphasis should not suppress the freedom of the Spirit.

It appears that the pattern of the early worship tended to be developmental and gradually evolved into specific forms. The influence of

Jewish worship tended to be a constant threat as new converts brought their religious experiences and patterns with them into the Christian community. The necessity of correcting worship forms that were contrary to what the apostles perceived as acceptable was an effort to maintain a balance between sound doctrine and freedom of the Spirit.

Worship, then, to the early Christians represented a relationship between God and His people. This relationship was rooted in historical redemptive events as evidenced by the creeds, sacraments, prayers, preaching, and the teaching. But above all, worship was possible because of the activity of the Holy Ghost that gave revelations, inspiration, and power.

CONTEMPORARY WORSHIP

Is there any continuity between worship today and the historic patterns of yesterday? Would the first century Christians recognize the patterns of public worship today? Of course, the worship space is vastly different today with air-conditioned, well-lit, and splendidly designed architectural structures. Putting aside the technological mega-shift between the centuries, is there any similarity in the content and spirit of worship? For, after all, our pattern for worship is a historic one.

Our contemporary worship must constantly be evaluated for content and Spirit. Content speaks of the doctrinal and theological correctness of what we say and do in the worship experience. A public service punctuated with prayers, creedal statements, readings from the Psalms, hymns, revelations, the Eucharist, and Biblically based preaching and teaching would reflect some continuity with our historical model. And of course, the freedom of the Holy Ghost to interact with the congregation and leaders would authenticate the experience.

Worship should be inspirational and informational. It should stir our emotion while also informing our minds about the nature, purpose, and will of God in Christ. Maintaining a critical balance between the emotional and informational content of the worship experience should be a goal of every service.

Public worship should be participatory. Every opportunity should be given for the congregation to be involved in the singing, offering of praise, and celebrating. Choirs, ensembles, and special musical groups are wonderful accompaniments to the worship experience, but they can in no way substitute for the rich expression of congregational participation. Of course, this is best achieved by the careful selection of the music and the content of the worship event.

Public worship should be orderly. A local assembly may have a rich heritage of different human expressions of singing, shouting, hand clapping, and dancing among the congregation. Those differences represent a reflection of the different religious histories of the members. However, the edification of the entire assembly must be held in balance with the benefit derived by each individual participant. Whatever is done in a public service should be for the edifying of the entire community.

A local Church may demonstrate tremendous love, gifts, and excellence in ministries and not grow. There may be tremendous preaching, teaching, and corporate worship, while the congregational dimension of the Church increases and decreases. What accounts for such a paradox? Why does a seemingly effective Church have to constantly be faced with congregational "turnover"? Let us begin with the religious history of most congregational members. If the greatest percentage of members of most congregations consists of individuals who have transferred from other ministries and a smaller percentage are new converts, then there is a great possibility that the spiritual climate of most Churches is influenced by a variety of different denominations. If a majority of Christians reside in Churches that are different from the Churches where they experienced salvation, this may explain the spiritual and emotional conflicts that occur in many Churches during times of corporate worship. Human beings can be influenced or "scripted" by their religious environment (see chapters 3 and 4). The behavior and mannerism that is exhibited by individuals during times of corporate worship are an emulation of what they have either seen or heard.

The religious history of congregational members can have a significant influence on their psycho-physical responses. This is true of Pentecostal, Charismatic, Baptist, Methodist, Lutheran, Episcopalian, Catholic, Independent, and any other denominational group. Since each denomination tends to cultivate and reinforce a particular human response to God during times of their public worship services, it is expected that the congregations will respond according to the acceptable standards and rules governing such human conduct. If there is censorship or freedom, the individual worshiper in each denominational setting will eventually conform to the prevailing patterns of response.

Many Churches today have congregations that were not converted under their denominational banner. Hence, most congregations are a mixture of many different denominational backgrounds. And in any particular Church, every group of new members brings their particular religious heritage with all of its forms and patterns of worship and governmental understanding. On any particular Sunday morning, any local Church will give a heterogeneous congregation consisting of vocally expressive, physically active members and those who are less responsive and even quiet. Since worship is individual and corporate, one of the objectives during times of corporate worship is to provide an atmosphere of individual freedom while not violating the rights of the whole congregation. For example, during a time of corporate worship in a large conference I was attending, a young man in the congregation began to give a very lengthy "prophecy." As I listened and observed, the entire mood of the service changed. Gradually, the people surrounding the young man began to quiet down until the majority of the congregation had been silenced by this interruption. As the leaders in charge of the meeting became aware of the young man speaking, they likewise became silent. The tone in which the young man spoke was very harsh and the content of the message was corrective, demanding the entire congregation and leaders repent of their sins. Since no one made an effort to hinder this activity, he was allowed to speak for approximately a minute. Once he finished, there was sporadic applause and shouts of affirmation from among the congregation. A few people shouted out, "Touch not the anointed." There was no response from the leadership of the conference seated upon the platform. They did attempt to reestablish the spiritual climate that preceded the interruption but were not quite able to accomplish that goal. The service continued with singing and later the speaker was introduced.

Such activity is not uncommon in some Pentecostal or Charismatic meetings where congregational liberty is encouraged. Members are motivated to express themselves by dancing, shouting, clapping of hands, leaping, and even running. And when the entire congregation is engaged in such responses, there can be some sense of corporate edification. However, there comes a time in the life of every worshiping community when a disruption of the service occurs that is not edifying nor comforting, but very distracting. It usually occurs when one or more individuals get out of symphony with the entire congregation or assumes a liberty that is not given to them. Such a moment can be beneficial to the entire congregation if it is managed properly by the leadership. But if such interruptions have a frequency of occurrence in the same congregation without being properly managed by the leadership, then there develops an "unsettledness" among the congregation and an atmosphere of "lawlessness" is perpetuated. And whenever leaders are reluctant to manage the corporate meetings of the Church, the uncontrolled behavior of a few members can have a very negative effect upon the entire congregation. It can cause a decline in the number of potential new members visiting the Church.

Leaders must be willing to manage the worship service and ensure that a proper balance of order and freedom be maintained. The numerous human expressions exhibited during times of public worship should be evaluated on the basis of their fruit. When the congregation is consistently made aware of the validity of their worship, their growth can be assured. Several questions may be helpful in such an evaluation:

1. Does the individual worship experience promote spiritual, emotional, and intellectual growth?
2. Are there any healing benefits to the individual's body, mind, or soul?
3. Does the experience build the faith, hope, and confidence of the participant?
4. Does the experience develop an addiction or dependency in the individual?
5. Is the experience a form without the involvement of true Pentecostal power?

The answers to these and similar questions can be helpful to the congregation and leadership in assessing singing, dancing, slaying in the spirit, laughter, shouting, and a host of other human expressions.

Every worship service ought to be evaluated by the leadership for its Biblical normalcy. A good rule would be to address the following parameters:

1. Content
2. Balance between emotion and knowledge
3. Relationship between the duration of time given to preaching, teaching, and singing
4. Nature and type of musical selections
5. Congregational participation
6. Holy Spirit involvement
7. Edification of the entire congregation

It is my firm conviction that a constant monitoring of these factors may provide continuity with our rich Christian heritage while providing freedom for contemporary expressions. If the worship experience is monitored, then the culturalization of worship and the various individual expressions and preferences will be subordinated to a pattern that is edifying for the entire community. This seems to be compatible with apostolic tradition (I Corinthians 12-14). And then the hour will come when the true worshipers will worship the Father in Spirit and in truth!

CHAPTER 8

Discerning the Role of the Church

What is Church? Why did God design and create the Church? What purposes should the Church serve in contemporary society? Several years ago I surveyed the new members joining our local Church, It was a time when our membership of approximately four thousand was increasing at a rate of one hundred new members a month. Our ministry was aired regularly on Christian television, and the Church was very active in the local community and offered programs for children, teenagers, the elderly, and the family. The public ministry of the Church on Sunday morning was outstanding with the preaching, teaching, intercessory praying, and the corporate singing and praising. The use of choirs, an orchestra, dramatic presentations, and choreographed dancing added a new dimension to the worship experience. So there were many obvious reasons to be attracted to such a ministry. But I wanted to know specifically why thousands of visitors came annually to our Church and why approximately twelve hundred of those visitors decided to become members. They came from different racial, ethnic, and cultural backgrounds and included the rich and the poor. Their previous religious history ranged from Evangelical, Protestant, Pentecostal, and Charismatic to Roman Catholic. Some of the reasons they gave for joining were:

1. Friends and relatives who attended our Church
2. Availability of social activities for singles, children, and adults
3. Preaching, teaching, and Bible study
4. Get in touch with God, inner communion with the Holy Ghost
5. To develop spiritually and experience the gifts and power of the Spirit
6. To be healed of physical and emotional problems
7. Close proximity of the Church to their residence
8. Friendliness of the members
9. The interracial aspect of the Church
10. The television broadcast of the worship service

The survey, although crude, raised suspicion in my mind concerning the nature of the Church. Could their motivations for joining a local Church reflect their concept of Church? Whatever assumptions and presuppositions people form concerning the Church will greatly influence their expectation, attitude, and behavior regarding the Church. And if those ideas about the Body of Christ are contrary to the Biblical model of the Church, it would explain, in part, the various dimensions of human behavior and attitude regarding the Church. And it would hopefully give some insight into the unrealistic expectations and demands that are placed upon the Church by its members.

The Church has to do with people and congregations. It is a corporate body of redeemed people out of every nation, race, ethnic group, family, tribe, and language. This is the sociological aspect of the Church. In the chapter on Body Life, we reviewed this sociological dimension of the Church as a people worshiping and serving God. But there is a theological dimension of the Church, which validates the authenticity of any group calling itself "Church." To summarize the Apostle Paul, the Church is the mystical Body of Christ, visible and invisible, heavenly and earthly, and historic, present and future. It is not a purely human thing, but a creation of Divine authority, which is present and operating in the power of the Holy Ghost who represents the presence of Christ. The Church is a custodian of the revelation and grace of God and a corporate representative of Divine authority in the earth. The Church is a redemptive people, energized by the Holy Ghost, directed by the Word of God, and called to be a doer of the work of restoration and reconciliation.

The Church, according to this concept, is not simply a collection of isolated individuals with separate and distinct social, cultural, and ethnic derivations. In fact, this community of people cannot be identified with any particular culture, political system, human ideology, or socioeconomic group. Its Biblical validity rests in its relationship with Christ rather than the inter-personal relationships of its members. Therefore, individuals who join a Church because of the racial composition of the congregation or because of other sociological factors must become aware that these characteristics should not be the most compelling requirements for their membership.

Our concepts and presuppositions concerning the Church cause us to be attracted to different models of the Church. Avery Dulles, a Catholic theologian, wrote a very insightful book entitled Models of the Church.[1] In this search of a theology of the Church, he brings forth the proposition that different concepts of the Church can be explored by using the explanatory tool of models. He presents the Church as an institution, a mystical communion, a sacrament, a herald, and a servant. The evaluation of each model is based upon Biblical and historical traditions and the personal benefits each model presents to the perspective member. There is an evolving conclusion that when the corporate Church performs certain functions, whether it be worshiping, preaching, teaching, healing, comforting, counseling, reconciling, entertaining, or providing social services to the community, perspective members are attracted by the ability of that function to fulfill needs in their lives. This certainly may explain the phenomenal growth that some Churches have experienced in this decade. However, the popularity of Church does not necessarily grant it Biblical validation.

The late Bishop Earl Paulk of the Cathedral of the Holy Spirit presented a concept of the Church as a prophetic community.[2] This concept is best described as a counterculture or an alternative society. It finds its Biblical support in the many examples of believers who committed their lives to Jesus and His teachings. This historical community of disciples with their exceptional lifestyles, values, and hopes was a constant reminder to the rest of the people of the transcendent values of the Kingdom of God. This concept has considerable support from the Old Testament examples of God's people being called by a prophetic voice to repent and to live in faithfulness to the covenant.

The concept of a counterculture or an alternative society seems provocative since it seeks to challenge, or at best, to influence the structure of the present society with values and principles signifying the rule of God. In this model, there is a strong concern for the social challenges of poverty, oppression, and victimization. God's reign is something to be experienced and embodied now in the Christian community. This model does not call for a withdrawal from the world, but for a new social reality and an actual social community with values and ethics in contrast with the existing society.

The preaching of the prophetic community is not primarily evangelistic. While salvation of the individual is a fruit of sound theological ministry, the emphasis is not simply to prepare souls for heaven, but the emphasis is for responsible priesthood. The preaching is prophetic while seeking to discern the times and to bring the wisdom, knowledge, and guidance of God into the present culture. This concept of the Church is socially active with its relevant programs and outreach missions. Activity follows the preaching in this concept.

In this model there is a "now" reality to the Kingdom of God without violating its "future" dimension. The Church is a microcosm of a society ordered by the principles of God's rule. Its members are involved in every legitimate facet of society including education, science, politics, law, athletics, economics, arts, and communication. The members seek to "live the gospel," not in communes or isolated conclaves, but in the midst of present society. Being an effective witness of Biblical principles of justice, righteousness, peace and joy is not simply proclamation, but it is a visible demonstration.

The Church as a prophetic community seeks to influence sociopolitical processes and structures. Its members, while not residing in the same geographic area, are linked together by a common faith in Jesus Christ, the Scriptures, and the belief that human effort can effectively cooperate with the Holy Spirit to bring about change. As the Gospel is lived out in a practical way in the midst of the present society, the Church becomes a redemptive community. As the prophets stood as a "witness" to the prevalent cultures of their day, so this model stands as a theological and practical witness. Influence and solution-oriented programs are weapons of practical warfare rather than force. This concept affirms the reign of God both now and in the future. It comprehends the polarities of the cross as both weakness and death, but also resurrection and power.

In discerning the role of the Church, the dimension and identity of the Church can be seen as the corporate body of redeemed saints, the mystical bride of Christ, but also as the present day agent of redemption, restoration, and reconciliation. The Church can be seen as God's authority in the earth and as a representative of Divine standards, principles, and lifestyles by which existing cultures, systems, and institutions can be measured and judged.

It is possible to reassess our assumptions and presuppositions concerning the Church. Now that some insight is given concerning the mission of the Church, it becomes possible for leaders to prioritize the essential issues of the faith in their preaching and teaching. Perspective members will not look first at the racial, ethnic, economic composition of the Church before joining. Hopefully, they will not exclusively consider the personal benefits to be derived from their membership. Leaders can now see the possibility of their local assembly being a redemptive influence in the community. We will further explore all of these areas in the next section.

Notes

[1] Avery Dulles, *Models of the Church* (Image Books, Garden City, NY, 1978)

[2] Earl Paulk, *The Prophetic Community* (Destiny Image Publishers, Shippensburg, PA, 1995)

CHAPTER 9

Alignment of the Church and the Kingdom of God

There has been no topic of Biblical research that has evoked as much controversy or given occasion to more debates than the issue of the Kingdom of God. All factions generated by this controversy agree on the existence of the Kingdom of God, but differ in their understanding of its nature, present implications, and time of its appearance. It is viewed as being future hope, present spiritual blessing, or some transformed state of existence to be anticipated.

The mystery of the Kingdom of God is that it involves a lot of things not yet fully understood. There are plural meanings of the Kingdom that breed confusion to the natural mind when efforts are made to circumscribe it into a singular concept. For example, the Kingdom of God is Divine action, but it also involves human participation; it is in some dimension now, but it is also future. These different dualities of meaning must be held in some proper balance.

Howard Snyder in his book "Models of the Kingdom" presents an excellent treatise of the different dimensions and polarities of the Kingdom.[1] His categories offer a meaningful solution to some of the controversy: (1) present and future; (2) spiritual and physical; (3) individual and corporate; (4) immediate and gradual; and (5) heavenly and earthly. Snyder's treatment of these polarities of meaning allows for conciliation between those who advocate the Kingdom as purely spiritual, future, and heavenly with those who see its present, physical, and earthly dimension.

Any effort to preach and teach the Kingdom of God without maintaining some connections between these extremes of meaning will result in serious controversy. Furthermore, a clear distinction must be made between the Church and the Kingdom. Jesus said, "I will build my Church" (Matthew 16:18). But He encouraged the disciples to pray, "thy Kingdom come" (Matthew 6:10). The Kingdom of God speaks of government and laws. The Church speaks of people, congregations, and worship. The Church is the earth station of the Kingdom as it propagates the principles and concepts of Divine rule.

The issue of "now" or "later" in regards to the Kingdom of God and the ministry of the Church is quite significant.[2] It is to be noted that the burden of Apostolic preaching recorded in the book of Acts and the Epistles was not upon future events. The critical attention of the Apostolic preaching was that God had visited and redeemed His people as evidenced by the birth, ministry, crucifixion, resurrection, ascension of Christ, and the pouring out of the Holy Ghost. Reference was made to the Second Coming of Christ, but the primary burden was that Christ had come (Acts 3:20-21, 10:42). The good news was that the Gospel was the "power of God unto salvation," and the Gospel was the hope of the nations (Romans 1:16). The hope of national salvation is now and not future. The Second Coming of Christ is the damnation of any who have not believed the Gospel for "now is the day of salvation" (Matthew 24:14, 25:1-13; Luke 1:76-79; II Corinthians 6:2).

The Second Coming of Christ is not the significant fact to which all else is preparatory; it is the confirmation that the finished work of Christ itself had supreme value.[3]

The death and resurrection of Christ signifies the transition from "the evil age" to "the age to come." Whatever events the Old Testament prophets may have referred to as coming are fulfilled in the birth, death, resurrection, and ascension of Christ.[4] The "age to come" had come.

In the Pauline epistles, the "new creation" has already occurred (II Corinthians 5:17). Believers have already been delivered from the power of darkness and "translated into the Kingdom His dear Son" (Colossians I: 13). The rebirth of the believer has already occurred (I Peter 1:3, 23), and they have already "tasted the powers of the Age to come" (Hebrews 6:6). The crisis of history is not future but past.

To lay the greatest stress upon the future in our preaching, teaching, and believing is to devalue the significance of redemptive history. An undue emphasis upon the events of the Second Coming of Christ at the expense of the First Coming is to place the believer in a state of complacency waiting for a cataclysmic event to occur which supposedly will bring deliverance and victory. It is possible that the thought of judgment to come may provide some strong motive to watch and pray for "the day of the Lord cometh as a thief in the night." But a focused attention upon the glory to come, while diminishing the significance of the present day with its duties, opportunities, and social claims is to breach the Gospel's demands for human responsibility.

To preach Christ as Savior and not emphasize the present day implication of His universal Lordship would focus the work of the preacher upon the salvation of souls for a future heavenly kingdom rather than the preparation of laborers for today. There must be a proper relationship between heavenly rewards and present day responsibilities. Salvation is not only the liberation from bondage, but also the engagement of a productive life. The social and ecological claims of salvation precede the heavenly rewards. The salvation of souls may be the center of God's will, but it is not the circumference. There is an individual and a cosmic concern of heaven. And when Christ is preached as the Savior and Lord who came to reveal the will of the Father for the individual and all creation, now and in the future, then the interest of the Church and the Kingdom will be both now and later.

Conclusion

Now it is possible to see that when the concept of the Kingdom of God is correct, then the activity of the Church can be aligned properly. If the Kingdom is all future, spiritual, and heavenly, then the work of the Church will be primarily focused on individual salvation without much cosmic interest. If the concept of the Kingdom is purely present, earthly, and human, then the work of the Church will be mostly social, political, and economic, and it will address the needs of humanity without recognizing the depravity of an unregenerate world and the need for the power of God. The attitude and behavior of the Church is greatly influenced by its concept of the Kingdom of God.

Leaders should recognize that priorities in their preaching and teaching must include the principles, precepts, and strategies reflecting the present and future, spiritual and physical, human and Divine, earthly and heavenly, and gradual and immediate polarities of the

Kingdom. The following are some suggestions:

1. Reassess the Biblical content of the entire worship experience to determine if the preaching, teaching, singing, praying, and all celebration reflect a true model of the Church and Kingdom.

2. Re-examine all social programs for their capability to transform the lives of people into productive citizens.

3. Devise strategies for the Church to work cooperatively with local authorities, public housing projects, and neighborhood programs to bring solutions to the social concerns of the community.

4. Structure the Sunday school curriculum or the education classes to reflect this same agenda.

The perspective members seeking a Church community should not join fellowships simply because of the race or socioeconomic status of the congregations, but on the basis of the Biblical validity of the Church. The following suggestions are offered:

1. The Church should be receptive to all nationalities, races, and ethnic groups.

2. The preaching and teaching ministry should reflect the full counsel of God and not simply a narrow area of theological specialization.

3. Opportunities for members to serve without regards for race, nationality, socioeconomic status, gender, and age should be in place.

4. Worship should be both informative and emotional.

5. The freedom of the Holy Spirit and the love of Christ must be evidenced in the lives of members.

Needless to say, these suggestions are not exhaustive. Perhaps they may at best simply offer a place to begin in discerning our proper roles as members of the Church. As you add to the suggested list, continue to be discerning.

Notes

[1]Howard Snyder, *Models of the Kingdom* (Nashville, TN: Abingdon Press, 1991)

[2]George Eldon Ladd, *The Gospel of the Kingdom* (Grand Rapids, MI: Eerdman Publishing Co. 1977)

[3]C.H. Dodd, *The Apostolic Preaching and its Developments* (Ann Arbor, MI: Baker Bookhouse Publishing, 1936) pp.42

[4]Ibid.

CHAPTER 10

Summary and Guiding Precepts

Discernment is a tool of redemption. Whenever appropriate responses are made during times of crisis, potential defeat can be transformed into victory. The proper assessment of the environment of the home, market place, and the Church can be most profitable. In the preceding chapters, we have endeavored to cover a variety of different areas to validate the necessity of the tool of discernment in both the spiritual and the natural world. The following represents a summary of some of the guiding principles that may be helpful in the discernment process.

Discernment Defined

- Discernment is defined as the ability to identify and to understand differences.
- Discerning of spirits is the ability to distinguish among a

whole range of spirits that may be operating in a given space and time.

- Discerning of spirits is only possible by the Holy Ghost operating through the spirit of the individual. The term "discernment" is not limited to "spirits," but applies to every dimension of life that may require identification, approval or disapproval.

- Discernment requires some standards or principles.

Discernment and the Spirit Realm

- Human beings are complex creations, which uniquely combine the spiritual, emotional, and physical in the expression of being.

- Human beings are not without control of their behavior, and they have the power to change.

- Our orientation in life may have conditioned our patterns, values, and concepts.

- Decisions about personal relationships, economics, education, and other social concerns should be directed by principles and precepts that do not cause estrangement from Biblical guidelines.

- Salvation and the ongoing work of the Holy Spirit in the life of the individual is absolutely necessary to resist evil and to live a wholesome life.

- Biblical instruction should not be limited to prohibitions and notifications of the consequences of human failures. People need instruction in righteousness and in the issues of life in order to discern the way of good and the way of evil.

- Religion cannot replace the role of parents or family in providing value clarification, character adjustment, and role models, which shape human existence.

- Christian orientation may determine the foundation for the respect for life, law, and order, but the home is the place for early training.

- The spiritual world of angels and demons is a reality.
- There are characteristic activities and strategies of evil spirits that can influence and control humans either directly or indirectly through sickness, psychological disorders, and oppression.
- Evil spirits can narrow the conscious level, suppress the level of creativity and liberty, arrest personal, spiritual, and emotional growth and maturity, and promote a departure from Biblical beliefs, practices and attitudes.
- Whenever there is a departure from orthodox beliefs and practices, and there is isolation from the established community of family and friends, attention should be focused on the source motivating such behavior. Condemnation, feelings of extreme guilt, fear, and anxiety are not characteristic of divine activity.
- Human dysfunction such as disease and psychological disorders cannot be relegated simply to scientific explanation.
- Medical intervention, scientific explanation, and spiritual deliverance should all be considered in the management of human physical and psychological disorders.
- Spiritual counselors and the scientists should combine faith and medicine in the diagnosis and treatment of human problems.
- Symptoms of demonization and medical disorders can overlap.
- The ability of human beings to receive information through such phenomena as astrology, fortune telling, witchcraft, sorcery, ESP, and other paranormal sources is well documented.
- The power of the Holy Ghost as the communicator of divine wisdom and knowledge is distinctively different from such paranormal phenomenon.
- Public media, marketing advertisement, political and social ideologies, and the unconscious language of signs and symbols influence emotions, thoughts, values, and judgments.

- Generational beliefs and values are transmitted through family, friends, intellectuals, politicians, and even religious leaders.
- The environment of the home, school, market place, and the Church can greatly influence operational behavior and attitude toward people, places, organizations, and institutions.

Discernment and the Natural Realm

- Ideologies, concepts and non-verbal symbols are capable of influencing our values, choices, and behavior.
- Justification by faith does not deny the restraints of moral law.
- Concepts of human worth respect for life, and individual freedom should possess a permanent residence in the laws of every evolving generation.
- An act cannot be judged as right or wrong solely by the motive or intent.
- Over categorizing is a common cause of prejudice. The beliefs, standards, and behaviors of any dominant group is capable of influencing an individual.
- Denominational Christianity can represent the cultural traditions and norms of an ethnic and a racial group.
- The media and marketing may influence our concepts regarding race, culture, gender, and even age.
- Our experiences with people who are different than our selves can greatly influence our perception of an entire group.
- People are not the same in their values, behavior, and attitudes just because they belong to a certain racial group.

Discernment and Prophecy

- Only God has the power to declare a thing shall come to pass long before it is in existence, and to bring it to pass.

- Prophets are not infallible, and they possess personal opinions.
- All prophecy should be judged to determine its source, content, intent, and the appropriate response.
- Prophecy is not an independent source of divine guidance nor a substitute for wisdom and knowledge that comes from sound Biblical preaching, teaching, counseling, and personal experience.
- It is the responsibility of the individual believer to exercise discipline in the discharge of spiritual ministry of prophecy.
- All personal prophecy is conditional.
- Prophetic decrees and promises to the individual require faith, discretion, and participation on the part of the individual.
- The accuracy of a prediction, a word of knowledge, or word of wisdom does not, in itself, validate the source of such revelation as Divine.
- Personal prophecy should be kept in proper context and should not serve as the only source of counsel, knowledge, and information in making decisions and judgments.
- Prophetic consensus, like a multitude of counsel, should be considered to confirm directive or predictive elements of personal prophecies.

Discernment and Reformation, Refreshing and Religious Fads

- When neglected truths and practices are restored to a level of acceptance, there remains the possibility of an over statement and a neglect of other foundational teachings.
- Spiritual reformations are generally universal in their application, reproducible by faith, validated by some Biblical precept, principle or example, and capable of transcending the time frame of their initial occurrence.
- Reformations have positive (renewal and refreshing) and nega-

tive (prohibition and abolition) elements.

- True reformation activity generally precipitates unity, fellowship, and cooperation among the Churches.
- The human responses to the ministration of the Holy Ghost such a laughter, slaying in the spirit, joy, shouting, and other emotional and physical activities should not be the only measuring rod of a true visitation of God.
- Slaying in the spirit, laughter, joy, and many other human responses are valid responses during times of tremendous Pentecostal activity and should be managed properly.
- Emotional and spiritual experiences should be evaluated on the basis of their fruit and put in a proper perspective with the intent of the worship experience.
- The psycho-physical dimension of the worship experience should be kept in balance with the other ingredients of worship such as the ministry of the word, Eucharist, baptism, prayers, giving of tithes and offerings, acts of benevolence, and so forth.
- Fads represent a temporary intrusion into the religious or social environment of practices, principles, policies, and standards of behavior that deviate from the status quo.
- Fads are generally not universal in their application and cannot be reproduced by faith.
- The after- effects of these products of human ingenuity, imagination, and will are generally non- productive.
- Principles and practices that have no redemptive value and cannot be reproduced by faith should not be considered as a foundation for a ministry.
- Principles and practices should not be considered false nor rejected simply because they are outside of our sphere of orthodoxy
- Eccentric behavior and questionable practices should not be the only basis for invalidating a particular movement.
- Principles and practices that are sovereignly initiated and

terminated, geographically and situationally specific, non-exportable, and Biblically validated, should be considered as temporary times of refreshing.

- Principles and practices that are not redemptive in character, localized in their application, and not reproducible by the universal faith community should be carefully examined for their contribution to the growth, unity, health, and mission of the Church.

Discernment and Body Life

- The corporate worship patterns of the vast numbers of Christian communities reflect the influence of culture, religious background, and the numerous concepts of the worship experience.
- The atmosphere of the worship experience, the music of celebration, and the ministry of the Word in different Churches is not always comparable.
- The manner of human expressions and the various degrees of emotionalism during times of corporate worship is not genetic or peculiar to a particular race, but it is an acquired or learned behavior.
- The contents of worship such as the ministry of the Word, Eucharist, baptism, giving of tithes and offerings, singing, and the various ministration of the Holy Spirit should not be in competition.
- Corporate worship should be orderly and participatory. The benefit to the individual worshiper should not be at the expense of the edification of the entire worshiping community.
- Worship is a re-enactment of historical truths and concepts, and it should be constantly monitored for its Biblical content and intent.
- Freedom and order are both compatible during times of corporate worship.
- Worship should be emotional, inspirational, and informational.

- The worship experience can be evaluated for its content, balance between emotion and knowledge, relationship between preaching and singing, nature and type of music, congregational participation, Holy Spirit involvement, and the corporate edification.

Discernment and the Role of the Church

- The assumptions and presuppositions we have concerning the Church will influence our expectations, attitudes, and behavior regarding its ministry.
- The Church represents a corporate body of redeemed people out of every nation, race, kindred, tribe, and tongue.
- The sociological dimension of the Church represents people and their obedience to God.
- The theological dimension of the Church represents the Biblical identity of the Church.
- The Church cannot be identified with any particular race, culture, political system, human ideology, or socioeconomic group.
- Church membership should not be determined by the social, cultural, or ethnic composition of its congregation.
- The popularity of a Church does not necessarily grant it Biblical validation.
- The Church as a prophetic community represents a viable model of an alternative society capable of implementing the rule of God in the earth.
- Influence and solution-oriented programs of the Church are weapons of practical warfare.
- The Kingdom of God must be viewed as a comprehensive eschatological dimensions, human involvement, Holy Spirit ministration, and relationship to the Church and the world.
- The receptivity of the Church to all nationalities, races, and ethnic groups is the Biblical norm.

- The preaching and teaching ministry of the Church should reflect the revelation of the full counsel of God and avoid theological specialization.

Alignment with the Kingdom of God

- There are plural meanings of the Kingdom of God.
- A clear distinction must be made between the Kingdom of God and the Church.
- The critical attention of the Apostolic preaching was that God had visited and redeemed His people as evidenced by the birth, ministry, crucifixion, resurrection, ascension of, and the pouring out of the Holy Ghost.
- The hope of national salvation is now and not future.
- The Second Coming of Christ is not the significant fact in New Testament preaching.
- Biblical preaching should not put an undue emphasis upon the events of the Second Coming of Christ at the expense of the First Coming.

Conclusion

Preaching and teaching must include the principles, precepts, and strategies reflecting the present and future, spiritual and physical, human and Divine, earthly and heavenly, and gradual and immediate dimensions of the Kingdom.

APPENDIX

Discernment must take into consideration the sovereignty of God. The will of God as revealed in the Scriptures and through personal experiences (prophecy, words of knowledge, visions, dreams, reflections, etc.) should be taken into consideration during the discernment process. Common discretion should not be discarded since many issues that require discernment can be handled appropriately by applying practical wisdom (common sense). Principles and precepts that have served as the basis of our philosophy of life should not be violated during times of critical decision-making. Concepts and values that have been developed over years of experiences should be engaged during critical times of testing, evaluating, and judging of events, issues, and even people.

Discernment should often be a corporate event. A multitude of counsel should be solicited during such times. The opinions of other people can be beneficial even when those opinions are contrary to our own. Consensus judgment can often occur when the majority of opinions are the same. However, there are times when a consensus of opinions is lacking and discernment becomes a personal option. It is during such times that we must take advantage of the principles, precepts and values that have shaped our philosophy of life and even our philosophy of ministry.

Discussion Scenarios

The following scenarios are presented for the reader's evaluation. As a practical application of what we have learned, examine each case and write out your response. These can be helpful in creating some scenarios of your own.

Case 1

Bob attended a Bible study and received a prophecy from one of the teachers in attendance. The prophecy described a call to ministry and gave several steps of action that he was to take in obedience to the call. He was instructed to attend Bible school and join a certain Church for further instruction. Bob had never received such a "word" before and was perplexed because he had recently graduated from Law School and had joined a very good law firm. How should Bob respond? Should he disregard the prophecy? How can he test the prophecy?

References: Chapters 2, 4 and 5

Case 2

Mary has been exhibiting unusual behavior. She has always been a very deliberate and practical individual. Yet, she has become very irrational. She is often absent or late for appointments. Her personal appearance, which was always exceptionally neat, has degenerated. Her hair and clothing lacks the attention that she has always given to them.

Some of the friends at Church believe she has a "spirit problem" and needs to be delivered. Her close friend revealed that she has been under unusual stress because of some personal crisis. How should Mary's friends respond to her? Should they encourage her to visit a physician? Should a pastor or counselor be consulted? Are there signs of "demonic possession" evident? If so, what are they?

References: Chapters 1, 2 and 3

Case 3

Mr. Jones has been calling the "psychic hotline" every Wednesday night for a month. His wife thinks that this is witchcraft and sorcery and warned him to stop calling the "hotline." Mr. Jones feels that his calling is innocent. He has received some good information from some of his calls and thinks that psychics and prophets are identical. Is this psychic phenomenon or Pentecostal power? Does the "rightness" of the information received by Mr. Jones prove the source of the power? What do the Scriptures have to say about sorcery, witchcraft, and divination?

References: Chapters 2 and 3

Case 4

During a classroom discussion on prejudice, a question arose concerning some of the possible origins. Several of the students attributed any kind of bias to "spiritual oppression." As the discussion continued one of the students suggested that prejudice was the result of generations of beliefs, values and ideologies that have been passed on to us through family, friends, politicians, and even religious leaders.

Enter into the discussion and share some of influences of the natural realm upon our beliefs, ideas, values, and behaviors.

Reference: Chapter 4

Case 5

A local church has been experiencing an unusual "visitation." A visiting minister has been preaching every night of the week for a month and members of the congregation are being "slain in the spirit," while others are laughing uncontrollably. During times of corporate singing, many members of the congregation are dancing, leaping, and running in the aisles. The meetings have attracted many visitors including leaders of other Churches. The attendance at the local Church has increased so much that several services are scheduled each day to accommodate the visitors. Consider yourself in attendance at one of these services. How would you describe these events? Is there an appropriate way to evaluate the worship service?

References: Chapters 6 and 7

Case 6

The elders of a local Church have been attempting to integrate the congregation. They have invited guest ministers and choirs of other racial groups in order to attract visitors. The strategy seems to be successful for a while in attracting other racial groups. However, the visitors seem to attend services for a while and then eventually leave. Is this a good approach? What other suggestions would you offer?

References: Chapters 4 and 7

Case 7

A local, ethnically, and racially homogeneous church is undergoing a significant change in the congregation. Blacks, Whites, Asians, and Hispanics are beginning to worship together. Initially tremendous excitement surrounds the new experience. There exists a mutual accommodation and cultural interchange among the group. Different idioms of musical expressions are introduced.

Gradually, the cultural tolerance begins to diminish. Group preferences begin to surface, becoming more obvious during times of corporate singing. Ethnic and cultural responses to the different kinds of musical selections become obvious. Efforts to appease the musical requirements of each group become less successful. The elders and musical department are attempting to evaluate the entire corporate worship service. What criteria can be used in such an evaluation? Should the cultural and ethnic demands of the congregation be addressed? Are there greater issues to be discussed than the selection of music?

CPSIA information can be obtained
at www.ICGtesting.com
Printed in the USA
LVHW081349221119
637824LV00024BA/1193/P